STARBODIES

STARBODIES

The Women's Weight Training Book

Dr. Franco Columbu and Dr. Anita Columbu

with R.R. Knudson

A Dutton Paperback

E.P. Dutton   New York

Photographs by Robert Gardner, except for photographs in Chapter 9, which are by Art Zeller. Photograph for Exercise 70 in Chapter 9 is by Robert Gardner. Photographs for Exercise 49 are by Art Zeller.

For information contact: E. P. Dutton, 2 Park Avenue, New York, N.Y. 10016

Library of Congress Cataloging in Publication Data

Columbu, Anita.
Starbodies.

   1. Weight lifting.   2. Exercise for women. I. Columbu, Franco, joint author.   II. Knudson, R. Rozanne, 1932–   joint author.   III. Title. GV546.C64 1978   796.4′1   78–8667

ISBN: 0–525–47527–3

Published simultaneously in Canada by Clarke, Irwin & Company Limited, Toronto and Vancouver

10 9 8 7 6 5 4 3

To our parents:
Antonio and Maria Grazia Columbu,
Joseph and Nettie Santangelo.
We cherish their constant support and help.

Contents

Preface

Over their years as comic-book readers, as many girls as boys have probably glanced at that classic Charles Atlas advertisement, "The Insult That Made a Man Out of Mac."

Poor Mac. There he is now—forever —with sand in his face, a victim of "the worst nuisance on the beach." Mac stands beside his beach umbrella, vowing to get even. He pouts. His nameless girlfriend throws Mac a scornful glance. Even the sun seems to fade until **LATER.** Then Mac returns to his same beach blanket and girlfriend. We scarcely recognize him. He has followed the Charles Atlas method. He is no longer a "soft, frail, skinny, flabby, half-alive runt." With a strong right arm he's prepared to get even. He punches the bully. He impresses his girl, who brings a smile to Mac's sullen face with this compliment: "Oh, Mac, you *are* a real man after all!" She clasps Mac's new shoulders. She smiles with him.

Why is this woman smiling? She is soft, frail, skinny, flabby, the same out-of-shape blob, summer after summer, advertisement after advertisement. Her body has neither tone nor definition. Her waist is thick, her legs straight as sticks. The other two women on the beach are almost as shapeless as she is, but they also smile at the heroes around them, whose "tireless legs," "slimmer waists," "ironhard stomach muscles," "more energy and stamina," "more solid weight in the right places"—yes, and "more magnetic personality" have resulted from the Charles Atlas promise to make one who follows his program "A NEW MAN."

Women are promised nothing. Their flabby figures in Atlas advertisements are merely pale decorations, less alive than the flowers on their beach blankets. Generations of comic-book readers have probably never noticed that Atlas women could benefit from his program. If his men have a "Before" and an "After," why shouldn't his women? They seem to have only a "Never." But women, too, need slimmer waists, stronger stomach muscles, tireless legs, more energy and stamina, more *solid* weight in the *right places*—yes, and the stronger ego that follows as a result of a healthier, better-looking, stronger body.

Today women are beginning to feel a need not only for better-looking bodies but also for stronger bodies. Strength improves the stamina of working women. For teachers, saleswomen, doctors, secretaries, telephonelineswomen, army captains, and all other women on the job, stamina will make the day go easier on both body and mind. For housewives, strength moves furniture and children; stamina saves energy for evening activities. Strength improves skills for sportswomen: strength is speed on the tennis court; strength is power on the golf course; stamina takes a cross-country skier to the end of her course—faster. Strength repels mashers, muggers, and others' unwanted attention. Strength attracts wanted attention. For more and more women today, strength is beautiful.

Franco and Anita Columbu recognize women's need for strength, health, and beauty: an "After" to a fitness program. The pages to follow present the Columbus' weight-training programs, designed specifically for women. Every word of advice, every exercise and lift is based on the Columbus' thirty years (combined) of study, training, and experience with body strengthening and body building for both men and women.

Strength, energy, good health, and looks: birthrights for a fortunate few. The rest of us must strive for these goals. If you are willing to invest the time to follow the Columbus' programs, you will achieve almost immediate results. Nothing works faster to tone and strengthen muscles, to reduce fat, to proportion the body, and generally to improve fitness than exercising with weights. Half an hour—forty-five minutes—every other day will take you further toward being a New Woman than if you were to follow more time-consuming, gadget-filled, or trickier, faddish programs.

Begin by imagining your swift progress. And see your "starbody" now.

R. R. KNUDSON

Los Angeles
May 1978

STARBODIES

1

See Your Future Body Now

Stand and look at yourself in a full-length mirror.

First of all, choose the parts of yourself that you like best. Perhaps you like the thickness of your hair, your large eyes, and your unusually white teeth. You like your hands, their shape and size. You like how tall you are even in bare feet. Heredity has done you these favors. So far, so good. But while deciding on your best parts, your eyes can't help falling to your hips, which you think are out of proportion with the rest of your body. And your stomach—well, pull it in with a deep breath and hunt farther for positive features. You like your firm and shapely lower legs. You've worked hard on them. They get lots of exercise from running up and down stairs and from playing golf. Your feet look strong, planted on the carpet in a golf-drive position, but they feel cold. Poor circulation, maybe? And your face seems pale.

Sun and make-up will "cure" your face, and right now you might be planning to turn away from the mirror and improve your appearance in those two easiest ways: lie down and let the sun do it; spend money on cosmetics. Or combine several easy ways: spend money to have someone else apply something to your face or hips or abdomen. Go to a body waxer, a masseuse, a fad-diet doctor, a plastic surgeon, a thousand-dollar-a-week health and beauty spa. Seek advice, comfort, and help about your most troublesome "body problems."

Instead, return to your mirror and identify your own problems. Face them squarely. You've always believed, for example, that your waist is too thick or you've felt your breasts are too slumpy. You don't want your thin neck or your few or many extra pounds here and there and almost everywhere except on your forearms and lower legs. Well, that's lucky. Legs and forearms show more often than other parts of the body except the face, so you'll be showing off your fittest parts. But now, looking again at your forearms, you suddenly wish for a stronger right wrist to use hitting the ball harder in a racquet-ball game. When your fingers brush against the tops of your legs you automatically squeeze, testing your thighs for ski muscles. Your thighs aren't fat, aren't thin, but they don't feel toned and supple. Also, you have a pain in your lower back that you want finally to solve.

Improved appearance. Conditioning

for sports. Fitness. These are on your mind—on almost every American woman's mind nowadays when women have time and money to spend on themselves. As you walk thoughtfully away from the mirror you plan to do something about yourself, about *your own body,* something for sure this time. Something realistic. You'll exercise while watching TV perhaps. Or something more demanding: you'll buy a bicycle and ride it around the neighborhood every day. Or you'll do something that will work fast. Like fasting.

You begin to see your future body as you plan a program of self-help. Your mind jumps ahead, imagining results and at the same time wrestling with what action, precisely, will gain these results. Imagination shows you the tighter abdominal muscles that result from this exercise: reasoning tells you to put on your shoes while you raise your legs, thus making your feet heavier. Heavier feet are harder to lift, and your abdominal muscles quickly feel the extra effort. Your imagination skips far ahead to a flatter, flatter stomach; you lift your legs and wonder if some book might explain such "heavier exercises" for every problem part of your body.

This is the book.

Exercising with Weights

Many women have casually stumbled onto an informal system of exercising with weights. Success from leg raises in tennis shoes or in ski boots perhaps led them to arm raises using a book—a thick dictionary held with both hands: raising it from the floor, over the head, stretching the book high, lowering it to the shoulders, raising, lowering, while counting to eight or ten or fifteen.

Also in recent years, women have discovered professional weight-training apparatus at their health clubs and reducing salons. They have worked out on calf machines, lat machines, leg presses, which are stations of the Universal gyms—standard equipment in health clubs these days. A growing number of clubs are adding Nautilus machines and other more exotic devices for lifting, pulling, pushing—exercising with weights. Other women have stayed home and tried out their husband's or son's barbells or dumbbells just for the fun of it—and for conditioning, fitness, and improved appearance. Eventually, perhaps, they've become serious enough to run through the series of weight lifts that they found described in men's magazines or in weight-lifting manuals.

Lifting iron dumbbells. Pressing your feet against pedals on a leg-strengthening machine. Even pumping dictionaries. You are on your way to a new body.

Because weights work.

And here's how: the added resistance that weights supply to your exercises causes your muscles to work harder than if you were simply pushing or pulling or bending or lifting without weights. Muscles grow because they are forced to put forth more energy. As you demand more from muscles, they adapt to the stress by becoming stronger. In addition to strengthening your body you are burning calories, many more calories than if you were exercising without weights. Exercise burns fat. Not only are you losing inches by toning your muscles; you are also losing inches by losing weight.

Muscles

Muscles are your body's *main* support and comprise 40 to 50 percent of your weight. Their function is to cause movement in every part of your body, including the digestive tract, circulatory system, and the chest, diaphram, and abdomen during respiration. The 650 muscles in your body are named according to various movements they perform (*extensor*, for example) or according to their locations (*radialis*, for example) or according to their shapes, divisions, or origins. Muscles bend joints and straighten limbs; they rotate, turn upward, turn downward, raise, lower, glide, hold. In performing any given movement, muscles are known as the *prime* movers.

Fat is exactly the opposite, for it needs to be supported and moved. It weakens your body's structure. It causes extra work for your liver, kidneys, lungs —for all of your organs. For example, for every extra ten pounds of *fat* your body carries it must build seven hundred miles of extra arteries and veins. Five hundred more gallons of blood per day need be pumped than if you carried ten fewer pounds of fat on your body.

Many women believe that fat turns into muscle during exercise sessions with weights. Others believe that muscle turns into fat if weight-exercise programs are curtailed or discontinued. Both of these notions are nonsense. Muscle cells and fat cells cannot mix; they are completely different things. Exercising with weights burns fat, that is, causes fat cells to die. At the same time, muscle cells are reborn, activated, and stimulated.

Let's take an example from an often-asked question women have about their upper arms. Confronting a doctor or an exercise specialist, a woman might begin, "Here, what can I do about this extra flesh [or fat or flab]?" As she asks, she raises her right arm high and pinches the back of her upper arm with her thumb and forefinger. True, she can wiggle this flesh, and true, it sags when her arm is raised—a problem for many women. She is asking about the triceps muscle or lack thereof, and the answer is to build this muscle with weight exercises, which at the same time reduces the fat deposited around her triceps. This muscle responds quickly, almost magically to weight exercising. Very soon the raised upper arm is firm. No amount of wiggling will move the flesh there; however, the strengthened muscle will not "poke out," as women are afraid will happen.

Women's Muscles, Men's Muscles

Training with weights has not, traditionally, been women's "sport." Probably the main reason for women's reluctance to add weights to their exercise programs is their fear of developing bulging muscles: they don't want to look like men, more specifically like male body builders, whom many women consider too brawny. "If that's what weights will do to me, I'm not lifting a pound," a woman remarked to her muscular male instructor at a health club.

Women's fear of muscle *size* is groundless. They need not worry about looking like body builders, soccer players, male gymnasts, or even like delicate but muscular male ballet dancers. Women don't develop bulky muscles the way men do because women have a low level of the male hormone testosterone, which is what gives men the physiological tendency to become muscular if they exercise. Testosterone makes body builders "pump up." Women's sex hormone, estrogen, makes them more prone to acquire fatty tissue than muscle tissue. Physiologist Jack Wilmore, who conducted experiments over several years with women training with weights, concluded that these women displayed "no significant additional muscle tissue."

Again, exercising with weights will reduce stored fat and will strengthen and harden women's muscles but not

Weights work. Added resistance causes your muscles to work harder.

Anita and Franco Columbu train together.

greatly increase their size. In a pinch, women can train using a man's guide to lifting (such as *Winning Bodybuilding*), but they will not achieve the overall results they seek because men's programs stress power almost exclusively. Women want a slimmer, tighter, sounder body. They want to change their proportions and *then,* perhaps, increase their strength. Our programs have been adapted especially for women's needs. The exercises take into account that women cannot, until an advanced stage in training, handle the heavy weights that men routinely lift. Women should lift lighter weights but lift them more often (every day) and more times (repetitions) than men do for explosive power. Usually women want to concentrate on burning fat, which all women store in different areas (upper arms, buttocks, thighs) from men (chest, stomach). Our exercises for women take these differences into account.

Consultation with the Columbus

With your fear of outsized muscles dispelled and with our promise of certain and speedy results from the Columbu programs to follow, you are ready to begin exercising with weights. But before we answer the questions you will have about getting started, return to your mirror for a professional assessment and consultation with us.

Look more critically at yourself. Is your body tense? Obvious clues, of course, are squinting eyes, a tightness around your lips, tightly balled hands, and curled toes. A less obvious clue is the set of your shoulders. Are they level? Holding one shoulder higher than the other is often a sign of tension. Exercise reduces tension, and a sustained program of working with weights will give you a self-assured posture and noticeably more relaxed facial expression.

While you work with weights your face is exercised by the many different facial expressions you assume when making tougher demands on your body. Exercised muscles become tighter, preventing premature wrinkles. Your skin coloring will improve as well. Pale or sallow skin will be nourished by the better blood circulation that results from regular exercise. Fresh blood brings nutrients to the scalp, relaxing it. (Tightness in the scalp contributes to thinning hair and premature baldness.)

If your mirror reflects a neck that you feel is too thin or a neck with hanging fat, you should be cheered by the fact that neck muscles respond rapidly to the weight exercises we suggest in coming chapters. A thin neck will take on muscle definition; exercise will burn fat and tighten skin. In either case your appearance is improved, and the strengthened muscles reduce your likelihood of neck injuries from such accidents as rear-end auto collisions and falls while skiing. Your shoulders, too, will be strengthened against accidents and sports injuries by our exercises designed to build the three parts of your deltoid muscles. Strong shoulders are of infinite help in all sports, and, as for appearance, extra work on the deltoids will actually broaden shoulders, if you happen to think that yours are too narrow. Muscle tone in your neck and shoulders will go far toward improving your posture.

Your forearms, as two of the most "exposed" body parts, should be curved and firm, even when not flexed. If you feel that they are too soft or too thin, either condition can be corrected by exercising the flexor and extensor muscles. Also, as you look at your forearms, study your hands, especially your fingernails. Pale fingernails are often a sign of poor circulation. Exercising your arms will bring color to your fingernails

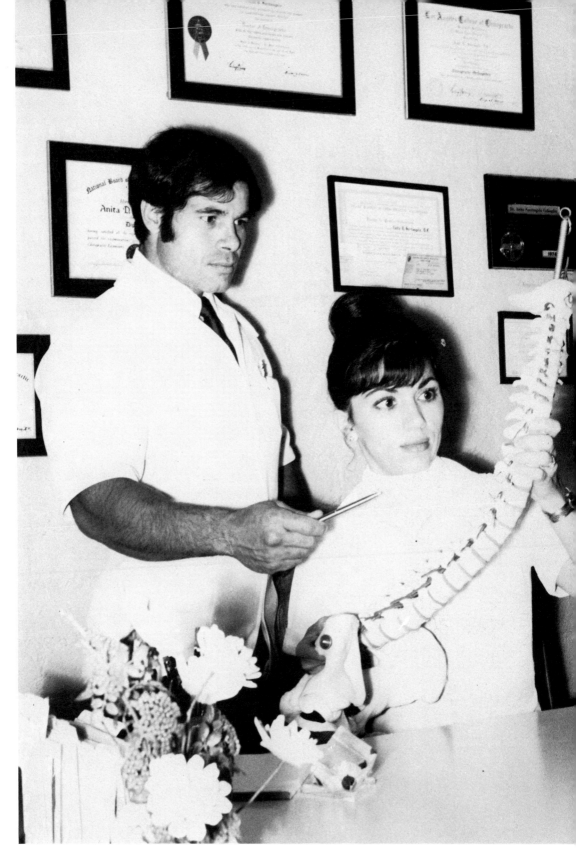

Consultation with the Columbus.

and strength to your wrists. Wrists play an underrated but vital part in almost every physical task you do, from tennis to housework to child care to programming a machine. Forearms give power to the hands. You will notice within a few days of beginning the first weight program that your grip is stronger: for opening bottles, for holding a bowling ball or a tennis racquet.

The biceps muscle, found in your upper arm, is the main muscle that men will roll up a sleeve to exhibit, proving their "athletic builds." Many amateur body builders devote most of their efforts to obtaining huge biceps measurements, possibly because weight exercises for biceps, especially at the outset of training, are easier than are exercises for other muscles: the biceps is already developed by yardwork and athletics. If you examine your biceps now you will see that, either flexed or relaxed, it will probably be more in tone than your abdominal muscles, for example, which do not get the exercise from housework, athletics, or professional work that your biceps receives daily. You should be encouraged by your present biceps tone. Flexing that muscle will demonstrate the tone that you will eventually see in your other muscles.

Perseverance is a key to the flat stomach and slim waist most American women wish for. The abdominal muscles demand more and harder work than others that are kept in tone by routine activities. For this reason we have included a variety of exercises so that you do not become bored, as you might have been doing the usual leg raises prescribed by other programs you may have followed in the past.

Now turn sideways and examine your back, the area between your shoulder blades. If this body part looks hollow, your muscles there (rhomboideus and levator scapulae) are weak. They need

building, not only for your back's sake but also because the rhomboideus and levator scapulae help support the shoulders, preventing a round-shouldered look. By exercising these back muscles your shoulders will straighten, improving posture and, indirectly, raising your chest muscles, causing breasts to be higher. Your breasts are glands on top of your pectoralis muscles. The glands' shape and size cannot be changed (except by reconstructive surgery), but in strengthening the pectoralis muscles you will achieve firmer, higher breasts. Like your abdominal muscles, your pectoralis need a heavier load of work because they are given less exercise in everyday life. Remember as you begin your weight programs that the muscles of your chest protect your body's most important organs, the heart and lungs. In a car accident or climbing fall, strong "pecs" can save your life. They deserve extra work.

Women who consult us about body conditioning ask most frequently for exercises to reduce their buttocks. Many report that nothing they have ever tried has helped them. Take a hand mirror and look at your buttocks from several angles. Fat is commonly stored there, it "settles," especially if you are sedentary. Of course fat can be reduced from any part of your body, but often the buttocks problem is not simply size but also position in relation to the rest of you: the buttocks tend to sag and appear flaccid if gluteal muscles are not in tone. Still, no matter what you might have thought in the past, the buttocks can be changed by exercising with weights. Like any muscles, the gluteus maximus and the gluteus medius respond to working against resistance by becoming stronger and tighter. If done conscientiously, our exercises will lift, firm, and shape your buttocks as well as burn fat stored there.

Strong legs are the foundation of a

A1: Biceps	**C1:** Pectoralis major (pectorals)	**E2:** Trapezius
A3: Radial flexor	**C3:** Deltoids	**F1:** Quadriceps
A4: *Forearm*	**D1:** Rectus abdominus	**G1:** Gastrocnemius
A6: Long palmar tendon	**D4:** Abdominus oblique	**G2:** Anterior tibialis
A7: Triceps	**E1:** Latissimus dorsi	**G5:** Soleus

Muscle groups: front

A1: Brachio radialis
A2: Long radial extensor
A3: Biceps
A5: Triceps lateral head
A6: Triceps long head
B1, B2, B3 Deltoids
C1: Trapezius
C3: Lattissimus dorsi
C6: Rhomboideus
C7: Erector spinae
C8: External obliques
C10: Gluteus maximus
D2: Biceps femoris
D4: Gastrocnemius
D5: Soleus
D6: Achilles tendon

Muscle groups: back

strong body. Without them your house-work takes longer, shopping seems end-less, you run out of energy on the job by early afternoon. Strong legs take you farther and higher while backpacking and cross-country skiing; legs win the second set of a tennis match. Yet few women ever ask us about leg strength during our consultations regarding their thighs and calves. They complain of thigh "bulges" or "baggy" knees and "shapeless" lower legs.

Weight training to strengthen your legs will correct these complaints and others you may have as you look in the mirror. A thigh that is made up of a little muscle and a lot of fat may have the same measurement as one that has firm muscle and a light layer of fat—but let's face it, it's just not the same thigh. Flabby thighs can become firm or even rock solid, depending on how hard you are willing to work. Shapeless, too-thin thighs can gain muscle definition and thus "fill out." Loose skin around the knees tightens with the stronger mus-cles. The backs and sides of your calves will take shape. Skinny calves will fill out. Seen from any future angle, your legs will be more beautiful if you exer-cise to make them stronger.

Try this small experiment for encour-agement. Stand with your legs together. Your calves should touch. If they don't,

they *will* after a program of Columbu exercises with weights. Your thighs should not rub when you walk. If they do, they *won't* after you have worked with weights in the programs to follow.

Our consultation ends with your feet. As you look down, remember they sup-port your entire body and that most American women do not walk far enough each day to exercise their feet nearly enough. Our weight programs give your feet a thorough workout. They will move in all positions while you ex-ercise the rest of your body. In learning to place your feet for lifting weights you automatically improve your posture. Your circulation will also improve: your feet will get less stiff while sitting for long periods and will not feel cold "all the time," as women often report to us theirs do.

Your body's weight, size, shape, health, energy, and strength are in some measure hereditary. Changes—improve-ments—can be made by working for them with weights. Before you begin, look at the muscle groups which are il-lustrated below. Women's muscles are in exactly the same places as men's. Al-though women will never develop mus-cles like Mr. Olympia's, the definition of his muscles allows you to see the place-ment of each of the muscles in your body.

2

Beginning

We have drawn together here the questions most frequently asked by women who wish to add weights to their exercise programs. We hope our answers set you eagerly on the new courses described in chapters ahead.

Q. **When** should I begin?
A. Today. Don't wait for Monday or for the first day of a month. These are not magic moments but simply traditional crutches to help you remember when you have begun a project. Write down today's date as your reminder, finish reading this chapter, and *do* the exercises described and pictured in Chapter 3.

Q. **Where** should I exercise with weights?
A. In your own home, in a room big enough to allow you to swing your arms and legs freely. You will need about eight feet of headroom. Or exercise outside in your yard, if weather allows, or in a section of your garage, where eventually a small gym might be established. Or, you might join a health club that has barbells and dumbbells *in addition to* its standard weight-training machines (like

Universal and Nautilus). Many women admit that the support and companionship they find at a health club keeps them from becoming bored with exercising. Others prefer to exercise home alone so as not to be distracted by the inevitable conversation and Musak that surround them at a club. Also, at home they are not bound to a health club's timetable.

If your basement or garage is large enough, you might consider sharing your equipment and know-how with a neighbor (or several of them). Friendly competition often brings out the best and most lasting efforts in weight-exercising programs.

Q. If I decide to exercise at home, **what equipment** will I need to buy?
A. You will need weights, which are sold by the set at almost any sports store and at large department stores. A beginner's set of 110 pounds will cost about $25 and includes a bar, two dumbbell rods, collars, sleeves, screws, and assorted weights (called plates). The dumbbells and barbell, fundamental pieces of equipment, are easy to assemble with the exact number of pounds

The calm atmosphere of a home gym is preferred by many women.

Dumbbell and Barbell.

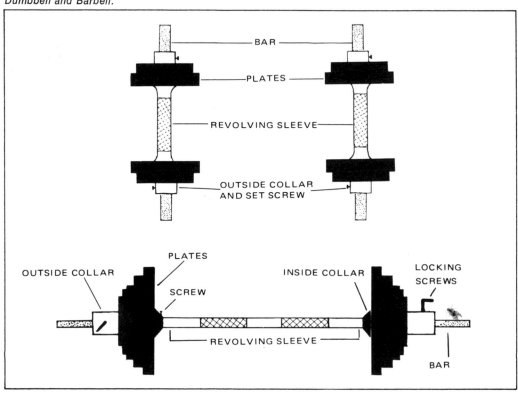

BAR

PLATES

REVOLVING SLEEVE

OUTSIDE COLLAR
AND SET SCREW

OUTSIDE COLLAR

PLATES

SCREW

INSIDE COLLAR

LOCKING
SCREWS

REVOLVING SLEEVE

BAR

for your exercises. You will understand at first sight the principle of interchangeable plates and with no help be able to attach the plates and tighten the screws with the small wrench which is included in a set of weights.

Adding or subtracting plates is what makes exercising with weights a superior method for shaping and contouring your body. Increasing the number of pounds you can lift and move will give you a sure record of your progress.

You may prefer to get started by buying only a set of dumbbells, the style (illustrated in Chapter 4) that is not adjustable. These will cost about $5.00.

Q. What if I decide to **join a health club** in order to use its special equipment?
A. There are no machines at any club that will tone and strengthen your body faster or more efficiently than will a $25 set of weights. Such home weights are cheaper than club fees for beginning and intermediate training. There are, however, other compelling reasons to attend a club: companionship, steam baths, sauna baths, swimming pools, etc. Not all clubs have weights in addition to their machines, so check for a rack of dumbbells and barbells before joining. Should you join, carry along this book each time and follow the programs we have developed for swift progress.

Q. What should I **wear?**
A. Wear clothing that is either loose fitting or that will stretch with your body movements: a cotton sweatsuit, an acrylic running suit, or a leotard and tights, for example. On warm days you might wear shorts and a light-weight shirt. On colder days it is best to have your muscles covered. Keeping them warmed up helps you progress quickly through the day's set of exercises and prevents injuries.

Because you will be striving to firm and strengthen your pectoralis muscles (those that support your breasts), it is best to wear a lightly supportive bra while weight training. If your bra is completely supporting your breasts, your pectoral muscles will not be working as hard as they must during your special exercises for them.

Q. **What time of day** should I exercise?
A. Weight-training specialists disagree on a "perfect" time of day for exercising, but we believe that afternoon hours between 2:30 and 4:30 are best. By then your body is warmed up and functioning well. Your mind is clear because the day's activities are almost over. But we realize that many of you will be unable to exercise in the afternoon and will have to choose another time that fits with your busy life. As you choose, follow these guidelines:

1. Try to exercise at the same time every day. Set a regular hour for workouts instead of cramming them into a choppy schedule;
2. Don't jump out of bed in the morning and start exercising immediately. Warm up first. If this is your only time to train, do some of the beginning program (Chapter 3) every day before you start the weight exercises;
3. With regard to eating: try to finish exercising an hour before eating or begin exercising at least an hour after eating. You will find that if you train on top of a meal you will feel sluggish. You will also discover that exercise tends to depress your appetite instead of increasing it, as many people now believe;
4. Try never to miss a workout. A rhythm is built up and maintained by exercising every *scheduled* day, a rhythm that is psychologically

helpful as well as physically exhilarating.

Q. **How often** should I train?
A. Do the beginning program (Chapter 3) for four days in a row. Then on the fifth day start the weight exercises in Chapter 4. The best schedule for you if you are overweight is to train six days per week. If your body weight is not a problem, alternate days of weight training with days of the exercises in Chapter 3.

Q. Should I **diet along with training?**
A. If you are overweight, dieting will help you lose pounds and inches even more quickly than exercising alone. (See Chapter 10 for information about nutrition while dieting and weight training.)

Q. What if I have just **had a baby** or if I am soon to have one. Should I be exercising with weights?
A. We cannot advise you about this because each individual is different. You should show your doctor our beginning weight program, and ask him or her when you can do some or all of the exercises. He or she should base his answer on the exercises and weights *he sees in the pictures.*

Q. Are there **age limits** to training with weights?
A. In East Germany and other Eastern European countries, extensive research points to *no youth limit* for weight training. Children eight, nine, and ten work with weights in Olympic sports programs. Their improved strength is a factor in winning at gymnastics, track and field, swimming, speed skating, and other sports.

Similarly, no present research places a seniority limit on weight training for women. Experience demonstrates that women can improve their strength and energy at any senior age. Women in their seventies and eighties are enrolled in weight-exercise programs conducted at YWCAs and health clubs across America. There is no reason why senior women cannot exercise with a set of weights at home, if preferred.

If, as a senior woman, you have doubts about weight training, we suggest you consult your doctor. Show him our beginning program, especially the pictures. Your doctor's answer should be based on your past and current physical condition *and* on our programs for self improvement.

Q. What if I am **menstruating?**
A. Studies based on women in the Olympic Games reveal that many of them set world records or achieve their own personal best performances during menstruation. This suggests that you need not restrict your own exercise during menstruation. Use judgment based on previous experience gained while playing sports during your menstrual cycle.

Q. **When will I see results?**
A. Almost immediately. Before you begin the first weight-exercise program, run your hands over each of your muscles, feeling for tone. Take the following measurements with a tape measure: upper arms, bust, waist, abdomen, hips, thighs, calves. After your fourth or fifth session, flex and feel your forearms, biceps, and calves. You will feel a difference this soon. At the end of your first full week with weights, take your measurements again. Your tape measure will show you a difference.

Q. What **goals** should I set?
A. Goal-setting in any exercise program is perhaps the most crucial element for sticking with that program. Without

daily, weekly, and overall goals you are tempted to exercise spasmodically or to stop exercising altogether if you are pressed for time and energy.

Set these daily goals: to complete all sets and repetitions of exercises according to the photographs and instructions; each day to strive for smoother movements; to strive for a slightly faster progression from exercise to exercise. In other words, lift more smoothly and rest less.

Weekly goals should be set by your measuring tape and mirror. Better to set modest losses in inches and pounds, for these goals can be more easily met than sterner demands on your muscles. An inch per month from your original measurements would be an average loss. At the same time, pay attention to the immeasurables: do you simply "feel better"—have more energy, less tension? Are you sleeping more soundly? Do you "look better" to yourself (skin color, posture, facial expression) and to others? (People are quick to tell you when you look better or worse!) Do your clothes "fit better" (slip on more easily, hang more comfortably from your shoulders and waist)?

Long-range goals are often plotted around social events: a party you want to be slimmer for or a bride's-maid dress you must fit. Beyond these dates are life-range goals: good mental and physical health, professional success, successful marriage and motherhood, skill in your sports, and so on. If you continue with a weight-training program you will inevitably notice that your body's super conditioning will contribute to all of your life-range goals.

Q. I have tried and failed at other shape-up programs. **Why will this one succeed?**
A. Weights are not "slenderizing" gadgets, like those advertised in women's magazines and on television. Weights are not part of a crash system to better health or your accomplices in some zany fad diet for "instant flab-free bodies." Weights, all by themselves, are a time-proven, research-proven resource for helping you make a better body.

Training with weights is the only way the body actually works harder than by doing simple free-style exercises. Working harder brings faster results. Because you will see and feel changes in your body so soon after your first session, you will be encouraged to continue, and eventually exercising with weights will be a pleasant routine in your day. You will find yourself looking forward to it, beginning today.

3

Getting Ready to Lift

The simple exercises to follow comprise an effective transition from a sedentary, inactive life to the beginning weight program described in Chapter 4. If you have not been exercising routinely for several weeks you should start with Exercise 1 below and follow this transitional sequence for four days in a row before you actually lift your first dumbbell. These exercises should take you no longer than fifteen minutes a day and should be done in sequence 1 through 8 without avoiding any movement that might seem at first tiring or difficult. (If you have been following a home or health club exercise program in recent weeks, skip directly to Chapter 4.)

Two weight-training terms need definitions: repetition and set. These are basic to every exercise in the Columbu programs. By "repetition" we mean each individual time you do the exercise. For example, we say "Backhand stretch . . . 12 repetitions." In other words, stretch 12 times. A "set" is a group of repetitions. We say "Do 2 sets of 12 repetitions." In other words, backhand stretch 12 times, rest; then backhand stretch again 12 times. The group of 12 is the set. Sets can be comprised of any number of repetitions. Most often 5 to 20 repetitions make a set.

Exercise 1: Backhand Stretch
   Stand on tiptoes with arms as shown in picture 1A. Snap arms backwards, elbows back as far as you can reach them, picture 1B. Do 2 sets of 12 repetitions.

Exercise 2: Standing Side Bends
   Look at the picture. Stand comfortably with your hands on your hips and your feet spread wide. Bend right to left for a total of 20 repetitions, 10 on each side.
   Do 3 sets of 20 repetitions (hereafter called "reps"). For toning the waist and upper hips.

Backhand Stretch 1A

1B

Standing Side Bends 2

Seated Stretching 3

Exercise 3: Seated Stretching

Sit comfortably with your legs spread as wide or nearly as wide as in picture 3. Stretch your right hand to the opposite foot, left hand to right foot, and so on.

Do 2 sets of 10 reps with a half-minute rest between sets and before going on to Exercise 4. For toning and conditioning inner and outer thighs, waist, upper body, and backs of the upper arms. This exercise also stretches the rib cage and oblique muscles.

Exercise 4: Bent Leg Raises

Lie flat on your back with your arms to the side as shown. Start in the straight position. Your feet will be slightly above the floor. Bring your knees to your chest, then push your legs out straight again. Do not rest your feet on the floor at any point in this exercise. Do 2 sets of 20 reps with a minute's rest between sets and before going on to Exercise 5. For toning and conditioning abdominal muscles and thighs.

Bent Leg Raises 4

Exercise 5: Bent-Leg Sit-Ups

You might not recognize the exercise shown in 5A and 5B, for unlike the old-fashioned sit-ups you remember from junior high school, these are done with your legs bent. Also you raise your body only halfway, as in picture 5B.

Bent-leg sit-ups are difficult at first but become easier swiftly. If you are unable to do as many as 3 sets of 10 reps, do as many as you can. Your impulse will be to stop and move on to an easier exercise. At the moment your mind says "Stop," do at least one more repetition, rest, and do one more set. For abdominal muscles. Fat deposits around abdominals make this exercise difficult. Bent-leg sit-ups prevent lower-back problems.

Exercise 6: Lying-Side Leg Raises

We show this exercise done on a bench, but it is done just as easily on the floor. Lie on your left side with your legs straight. Place your arms and hands as shown in 6A. Raise your left leg 50 times to its maximum height. Turn on your right side and raise your right leg 50 times. For waist, upper thighs, lower thighs, inside thighs, outside thighs, and side of the waist.

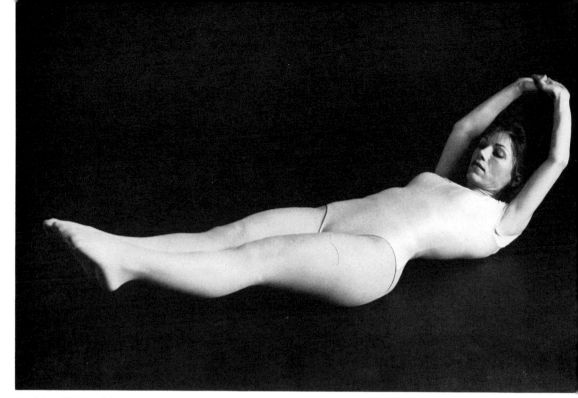

Bent-Leg Sit-Ups 5A

5B

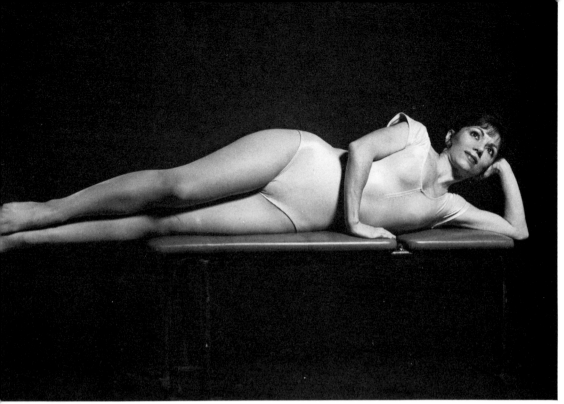

Lying-Side Leg Raises 6A

6B

Exercise 7: Hyperextension

This can also be done on the floor. Lie on your stomach, absolutely flat against the bench or floor. Place your hands as shown in picture 7. Raise your head and upper body until your lower back feels tension. Release to floor (or bench). Raise. Release. Do 2 sets of 10 reps for toning lower back.

Exercise 8: Back Leg Stretch

The starting position for this exercise is on hands and knees as shown. Bend right leg. Swing it forward a foot, then extend it straight back. Continue as in photos 8A and 8B for 2 sets of 20 repetitions with each leg.

After four days of bending, stretching, lifting, pushing, sitting up, raising, lowering, extending, and repeating you are ready to add dumbbells to your exercise program. If you continue to do these free exercises in addition to the weight exercises in Chapter 4 you will lose pounds and inches more quickly than if you train only with dumbbells.

Hyperextension 7

Back Leg Stretch 8A

8B

4

Exercising with Weights

This is the moment to pick up your dumbbells.

Unlike other sports equipment, they are not automatically appealing to your senses. The fresh smell of new leather golf gloves, the light touch of a steel fencing foil are missing. Dumbbells feel heavy and cold. They are usually black, sometimes rusty if you bought them second-hand. Compared to colorful surfboards and skateboards and dartboards, they don't cheer you with a profusion of stripes, zigzags, or stars. Dumbbells plunk dead if dropped on any surface. How to compare their dull sound with the agreeable pop of a well-stroked tennis ball? Moreover, you may feel like a sports slouch standing there in baggy sweatpants. Where are the stylish accessories natural to sailing, skiing, even softball?

Weight training doesn't need the fashion industry as a lure. Nor do dumbbells and barbells need color, although you might paint them yourself if that would cheer your lifting. The iron will soon warm in your hands. Dumbbells lose their ominous character after the first session. They will never feel like a balanced aluminum racquet, but they feel

more and more like ordinary sports equipment as exercise sessions pass. It's up to you to balance weights, to move them smoothly and with style. The simplicity of weight training may even be a welcome relief from competitive sports. After the tyranny of professional lessons, expensive equipment, and appropriate clothes, you will no doubt be refreshed by another approach to fitness.

The bench pictured in this chapter is not a faddish accessory. It is a fundamental piece of equipment for anyone who plans to make exercising with weights a habit. Benches cost about $30 at any sports store or large department store, and if you continue with our programs you might consider buying one for your home gym. However, an official, padded weight-lifting bench is not a necessity. You can improvise one with a garden bench, with several stools placed in a row, or with almost any bench you may already have around the house. Also, you may do the exercises on the floor or in a chair instead of on a bench.

In any weight program your progress depends on many factors. The ones we

Cross-Flys 9A

hope to control in your daily program are the specific exercises you perform, the number of repetitions and sets, the amount of weight used for each exercise, the time you pause between exercises, and the order of exercises. As you lift, remember these three tips:

1. Use at least 2 seconds to raise your weights. This prevents "throwing" them and causes you to work designated muscles.
2. Lowering is easier than raising, so you will feel an urge to "drop" the weight. Use no less than 4 seconds to lower weights. This emphasis will cause you to use the same muscle as you used to raise the weight. Be conscious of your form while lowering.
3. Exercise through a full range of motion. Thus the involved muscles retain their natural elasticity and joints stay flexible.

Exercising with weights is a self-starting activity and each session takes mental strength to "get around to" and complete. The added physical strength you feel almost daily, the swift improvements to your appearance, and the excited flush that comes with pushing yourself to the limit—these rewards should see you through our beginning program.

(The dumbbells pictured below weigh 5 pounds each. Use this weight for the first month of our three-month beginning program. For the second and third months use 10-pound dumbbells.)

This program is designed for three times a week during the first month (Monday, Wednesday, Friday, or Tuesday, Thursday, Saturday). After the first month you can keep training on this same schedule or increase your training to four days a week (Monday, Tuesday, Thursday, Saturday). The choice is yours, to be decided according to the progress you make during your first four weeks.

Exercise 9: Cross-Flys

Lie on your back on either the floor or a bench. Bend elbows slightly as shown in picture 9A. As you raise your arms, start crossing them (9B).

Do 1 set of 20 repetitions for the first two weeks; 2 sets of 20 for the second two weeks. After a month, do 3 x 20* to develop pectoralis muscles that support the breasts.

* Throughout, we will use this notation to indicate the number of sets and reps for each exercise: 3 (sets) x 20 (reps)

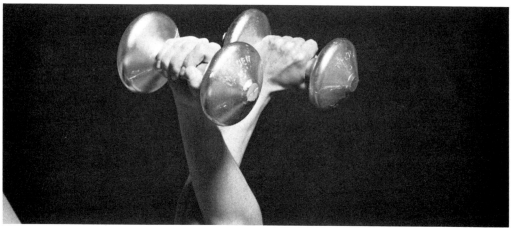

9B

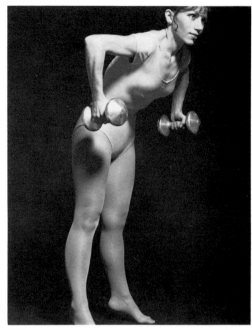

Bent-Over Lateral Raises 10A   *10B*

Exercise 10: Bent-Over Lateral Raises
This works the rhomboideus, which is
the opposing muscle to the pectoralis.

Stand bending slightly forward. Hold
dumbbells as shown. Raise them, draw-
ing elbows back (10B). Do 2 sets of 20
the first two weeks; 3 x 20 the second
two weeks. After the fourth week, do
4 x 20.

Exercise 11: Lateral Raises
Starting position: body straight, dumbbells held at sides. Raise dumbbells
slightly higher than shoulder level.
Lower them. Raise. Lower. Repeat 2 x 8
for the first two weeks; 3 x 8 for the second two weeks; 3 x 12 after a month.

This is *the* most important exercise
for shoulders. Strong shoulders improve
posture.

Lateral Raises 11A

11B

One-Arm Triceps Press 12A

Exercise 12: One-Arm Triceps Press

Sit down on any chair, stool, or bench. 12A is the starting position, elbow up and bent. Keeping elbow up, straighten the arm to point 12B. Repeat 12 times, then change dumbbell to other hand and repeat 12 times. The strengthened triceps hold flesh firm in the backs of upper arms.

> Do 2 x 12 with each hand for the first four weeks.
> Do 3 x 15 with each hand after a month.

Exercise 13: Wrist Curl

Start with your arms supported by a bench or other flat surface, such as a stool. Keep the elbows still and straight, as in 13A. Curl your wrists up as in 13B. Repeat to strengthen the hands and thus improve your grip.

> First month, 2 x 20.
> Second month, 3 x 20.

12B

Wrist Curl 13A

13B

Reverse Forearm Extension 14

Exercise 14: Reverse Forearm Extension

Exercises 13 and 14 both are excellent for the forearms.

Start with your arms supported by a bench. Turn wrists as shown in picture 14. Lift alternately, one up, one down. Curl no higher than the dumbbell pictured in right hand.

Do the same number of repetitions and sets as in Exercise 13.

Exercise 15: Dumbbell Squat

Stand with your heels on a block of wood, dumbbells at your sides (15A). Squat (15B), then up, down. Inhale going down, exhale standing up. Go down until your thighs are level with your knees.

The squat will firm your thighs and buttocks. It also helps to expand your rib cage, which gives internal organs more room.

First two weeks, do 2 x 12.
Second two weeks, do 3 x 15.
Second and third month, do 4 x 15.

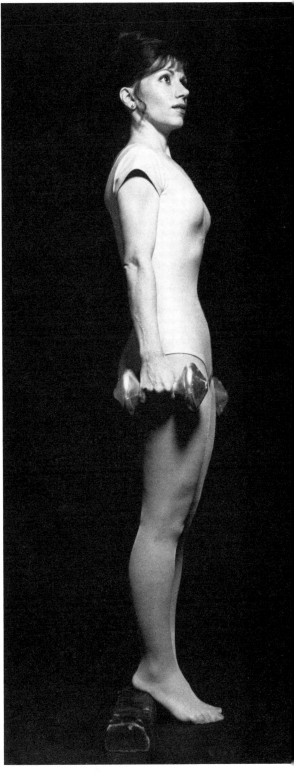

Dumbbell Squat 15A

15B

Exercise 16: Lunges

Lunges firm the thighs and buttocks and are good for all-around flexibility.

Stand up straight with a weight in each hand. Step forward as far as you can on your left foot. As you step forward, lower your body to the position shown in the picture. Your right knee will almost touch the floor. Raise for the pictured position, stand up straight again, put your right foot forward, and repeat the lunge phase of this exercise. Hold your head and torso straight throughout the exercise.

First two weeks, 1 x 2;
from then on, 2 x 12.

Lunges 16

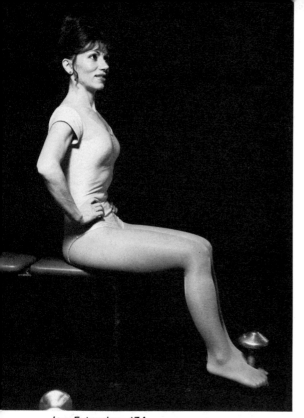

Leg Extensions 17A

Exercise 17: Leg Extensions

Leg extensions work the front of your thighs and help strengthen your knees against injuries. Begin seated on a bench or on a sturdy chair. Place your hands on hips or hold onto the bench. With legs bent, feet holding one 5-pound dumbbell off the floor 2 inches, extend legs to 17B. Repeat.

First two weeks, 1 x 15.
Second two weeks, 2 x 15.
Second month, 3 x 15.

17B

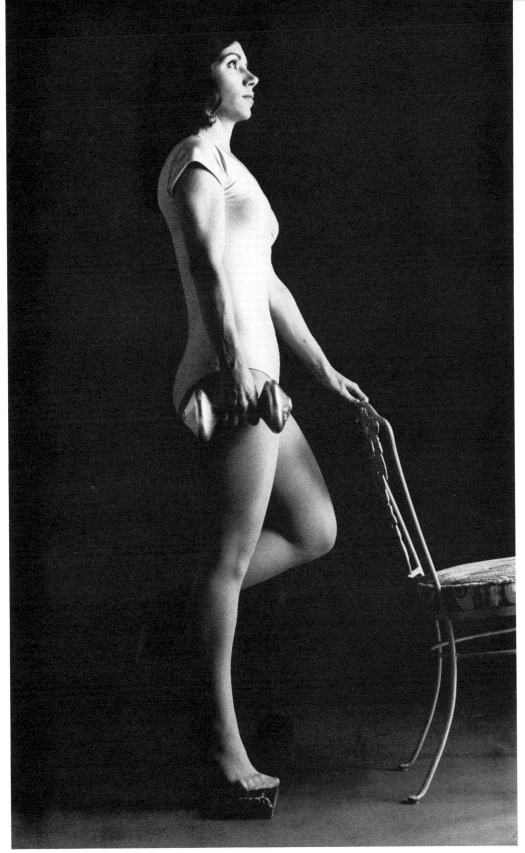

Calf Raises 18A

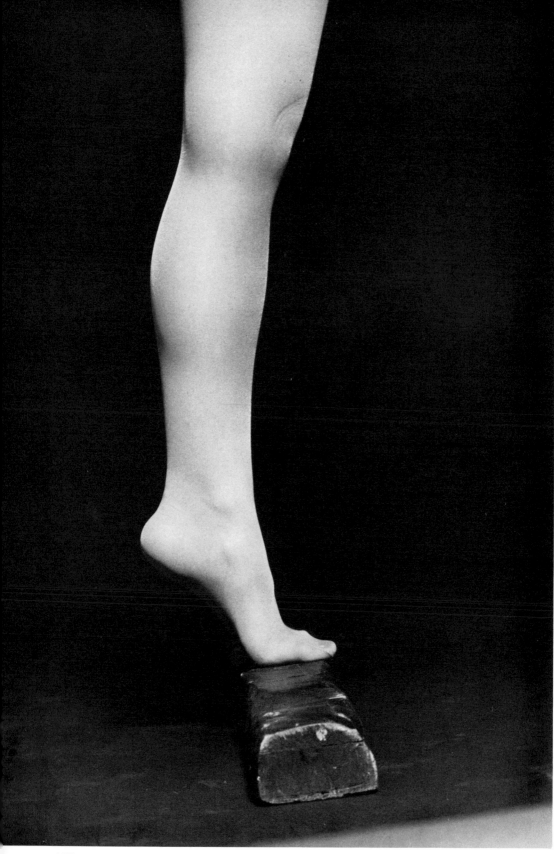

18B

Bent-Leg Sit-Ups 19A 19B

Exercise 18: Calf Raises

Stand on one foot on a block of wood. Hold onto the back of a chair for balance (18A). Go up and down on toes. Change legs. This helps to shape skinny calves or to firm flabby ones.

> Do 1 x 15 each leg the first two weeks.
> Do 2 x 15 the second two weeks.
> Do 3 x 20 after the fourth week.

Exercise 19: Bent-Leg Sit-Ups
(Same as Exercise 5)*

Bent-leg sit-ups are specifically designed to reduce fat in the abdominal area. They are best done without weights.

> First two weeks, do 2 x 15.
> Third and fourth weeks, do 3 x 18.
> The second month, do 4 x 20.

* Exercise 19, as well as other repeated exercises throughout the book is repeated because it is the *best* exercise for a specific body part.

Straight Leg Raises 20A

Exercise 20: Straight Leg Raises
Lie on the floor or on a bench. Keep hands in position 20A. Do exactly as shown in 20B. Every stage of this exercise is pictured.

Do 2 x 20 the first two weeks.
Do 3 x 30 the second two weeks.
Do 4 x 40 until end of program.

20B

Exercise 21: Lying-Side Leg Raises
(Same as Exercise 6)

If you are already doing Exercise 21 and Exercise 19 as part of your continuing use of the programs in Chapter 3, do both exercises in the order above, after you have performed Exercises 1–4 and 7–8 of Chapter 3 plus Exercises 9–18 of Chapter 4.

Do 2 x 50 on each side the first two weeks.
Do 3 x 50 on each side the second two weeks.
Do 4 x 50 on each side the second month.

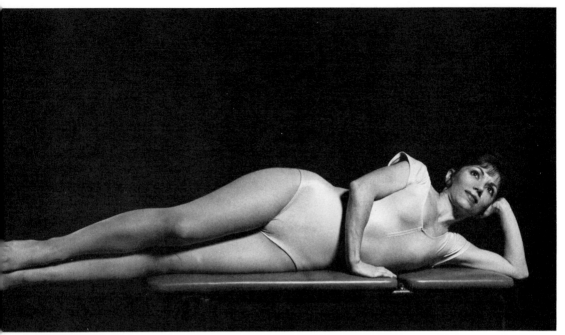

Lying-Side Leg Raises 21A

5

A Dozen Tips to Improve Your Training

By the time you have completed a week of our program you will be asking yourself dozens of questions about weights. Workouts provide a quiet pause in the day to think, and the feeling of enhanced mental energy that comes from more blood circulating to the brain will cause you to think with precision about what you are doing. Holding a monologue while exercising is not uncommon: "Am I gripping too hard?" you might wonder aloud as you repeat the dumbbell wrist curls. "Should I be writing down my sets?" "Where should I be looking during this set of flys?" You may also have told yourself that you're stiff and sore and bored, that you somehow can't concentrate on counting the repetitions. More than once you may hear yourself asking what you're doing with weights in your hands when all your friends believe it's crazy. Their ridicule might bother you.

Having been through the same self-doubting workouts when we first began training we know these troublesome questions need resolution before a habit of exercising with weights will be established. The suggestions below will help you carry on a more informed dialogue

between your two selves: the one who wants to continue weight exercising and progress in skill, strength, and endurance, and the one who would rather quit now, while the weights are perhaps still returnable. Concentrate on our tips before your next workout.

Concentrate Harder

Any book about any sport will tell you to concentrate while you throw, catch, pitch, hit, putt, lob, shoot, jump, and run. Coaches yell "Concentrate" at their players on field. But sports books rarely explain *how* to concentrate. Like the coach replying, "Just run faster," when asked by a runner how she might win her race, books leave the *process* of concentration for the reader to figure out. The instructions "concentrate harder" cannot help you have a better workout until you learn a step-by-step process.

Concentration stems from knowing your goals and believing in their importance. Start remembering your goals first thing in the morning. Remember that you want to feel better, look better. You want smaller, tighter thighs or a lower back that doesn't ache. Tense

To improve concentration, think about your arm moving through the full range of motion.

your muscles, relax, and think ahead to your workout. Think positively. Pre-feel the feelings you like best: the balanced, smooth metal weights; the sweat beginning to form on your temples; the flow of your warmed-up muscles as you complete the last set of exercises.

It is a physiological fact that your mind can dilate the blood vessels of an area to be exercised before it is even worked at all. Once the exercise begins, as much as twenty times the normal blood volume can be gained in the area. While you dress for your workout, concentrate on the muscle groups you will be exercising.

Exercising in front of a mirror lets you, observe your muscles working. Look directly at the muscle involved and try to see from inside. Visualize the muscle fibers and striations. These single fibers are bound together into still larger bundles. You are tightening, smoothing, strengthening the connections. Concentrate on that.

If you are exercising at home, don't answer the phone during a workout. Conversation breaks concentration, and in the time taken from weights your muscles cool down. Don't watch television to entertain yourself while counting repetitions and sets. Your entertainment should be feeling and seeing your muscles working. If you are exercising at a health club, try to avoid distracting conversation until *after* your workout. Concentrate on feeling the motion of exercise equipment interworking with your muscles.

Know the Meaning of Stiffness and Soreness

After a period of neglect—a long layoff from exercise, for example—the body loses efficiency in flushing fatigue toxins from muscles. Toxins such as lactic acid cause pain: muscle soreness. Also,

joints have stiffened because synovial fluid (the lubricating fluid found in the spaces in the joints) has not been moving through them efficiently.

You will certainly be aware of stiffness and soreness during your first weeks of exercising with weights, but instead of dreading the slight pain, you should welcome it as a sign of revitalization. Muscles are responding by firming. Circulation to the joints will increase and soon eliminate stiffness and permit your body a wider range of motion. You will notice your improved flexibility in every daily movement you perform.

With each new exercise you add to your schedule you can expect some soreness because a different group of muscles will be working. Also, when you add weight or repetitions to your usual exercises those same muscles will be working harder. Harder work causes temporary soreness until your muscles catch up to the extra demands. Even body-building champions and power lifters experience pain. In fact, they claim that a workout is "for nothing" if it doesn't produce muscle fatigue and afterwards some soreness. Next day, during their warm-up, soreness lessens to the point where muscles feel flushed and pleasant.

Never Wait for Your Partner

A partner in any sport can be vital to motivation. The companionship of someone with your same goals of improvement and persistence will stimulate you to stay with the daily routine, which alone you might find boring or too demanding or both. With someone alongside to evaluate your performance, you quickly and steadily reach your goals.

Unfortunately, a dependence on companionship can also slow your progress, for if a partner fails to meet you at your house or at the gym you will be tempted to skip working out that day. And the next, and the next until you are again side by side, urging each other on. Once out of your routine, it becomes easier to miss daily workouts. You will notice yourself using various excuses until you fall so far behind it seems futile to pick up weights again.

If you do find a weight-training partner, so much the better. Your next decision should be never to skip a workout if your partner doesn't appear. Further, you should begin your workout at the established time each day. Don't wait for your partner because you may run out of exercise time altogether if he or she is very late.

Warm Up Professionally

Notice weather, especially the temperature, and dress to keep your muscles warm. More warming up is required in winter and colder weather. Notice the condition of your body. Does it seem stiff or does it move freely? The warm-up should consist of the cross-crawl, followed by bending and stretching movements (as in Chapter 3). The cross-crawl helps balance muscles while tuning them up. As you lift your right arm, lift your left leg. Working in opposition (contralateral exercise) causes a momentary strengthening of all the muscles. If you work unilaterally (arm on same side with leg), your muscles get momentarily weaker.

During warm-up you will become conscious of your blood circulating in muscles, and your joints will feel less stiff. You are ready now for the first exercise of any program. Never skip a warm-up.

Follow the Columbu Order of Exercises

Every woman soon discovers that some exercises are easier than others,

in whatever exercise program she might be doing daily. Your own weight exercises will soon break down into "easy" and "hard" categories in your mind, and you'll look forward to the easy ones and dread the hard. You'll be tempted to take the exercises out of order, finish the easy ones first, perhaps, or the hard ones first so that you can look forward to the easier ones at the end of your workout.

We urge you to follow the order described and pictured in each exercise chapter. Working the muscle groups in the Columbu order is as important to your body as is the selection of exercises, the weight, and repetitions. In time, your hard exercises will become easy and your easy exercises almost effortless.

Exercising in a health club can present another problem in following the Columbu order: at peak evening hours, lines form for much of the equipment. If you stand long in line between exercises you are bound to cool off. If you decide to use only the accessible equipment you might be forced to abandon the Columbu order or to drop some exercises altogether.

If rush hour at the club is your only time to use it, you might consider buying weights and alternating every other night between home and club. Better, discover when rush hour takes place *before* you join a club. If that is your only free time to exercise, a home set of weights is a better investment.

Improve Your Grip

"A good gripper is a strong lifter."

These three methods of grasping a weight are basic.

Undergrip: Fingers encircle the bar from beneath with palms up and thumbs encircling the bar from above. The undergrip is used primarily in *exercises for*

The cross-crawl is excellent as a warm-up and warm-down exercise.

Undergrip.

the biceps and other muscles of the front upper arm, in which the bar is brought from thighs to shoulders and returned. The undergrip is not used in lifting a weight overhead.

Overgrip: This grip is used for all *overhead lifts.* Fingers encircle the bar from above with palms down toward floor. Thumbs encircle the bar from beneath.

Reverse grip: One hand grasps the bar in an undergrip; the other hand grasps the bar in an overgrip. Reverse grips are best for *lifting heavy weights,* usually from floor to thighs.

There is no reason (except indifference) to grasp weights incorrectly or to have a weak grip. Weak or incorrect grips cause numerous problems, including uncomfortable body positions while lifting, dropped weights that ruin furniture and floors, loss of peak lifting power, and injuries. An incorrect grip forces the body out of alignment during exercises. Strength will not increase as readily because the muscles of the un-

aligned area are not worked completely.

Squeeze the barbell. A sound grip develops stronger hands and forearms, tightens ligaments, places nerves under control, and gives you security while exercising. When your mind seems better connected to the weights you will derive greater benefits from a workout.

Breathe Correctly

In weight lifting, as in other sports, no detail is too small for consideration if you are serious about improving. When you first begin exercising with weights your mind will be focused on your hands, back, legs, and feet. You'll think "heavy." You'll think "up," "down," "nine," "ten." Counting repetitions absorbs your thoughts until you have established a comfortable pace. After that your muscles catch up with their load. You feel free to wonder about details. Right then you'll probably wonder if you should "breathe better," as long as you are

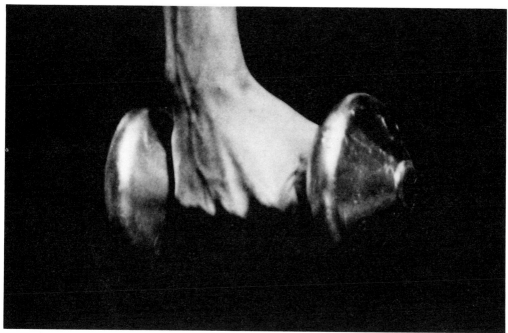

Overgrip

performing the other functions so well.

Good breathing habits during exercising will speed your progress. You should breathe deeply and rhythmically instead of taking shallow breaths or holding your breath or breathing spasmodically. Deep breathing improves circulation, thus sending more oxygen to the muscles being exercised. With more oxygen, muscles work harder. A deep breath will give you immediate vitality.

As a general rule, always exhale when the exertion is greatest during exercise. Inhale when you're resting, exhale when you're pushing or pulling or lifting (etc.) hardest. In other words, as you begin the exercise, inhale. At the point that the exercise makes its greatest demand on your body, exhale. As a general rule, breathe in through your nose, out through your mouth.

If you are training in a basement or in a small closed room, stop for a minute several times, go outside, and breathe the fresh air deeply. You will gain as much from this as a distance runner gains from occasional drinks of water during a race.

Watch What You're Doing

Every part of your body takes a specific position in weight exercising. Your feet, for example, have a range of stances from widespread to together. Your hands take shoulder-width overgrips, wider undergrips, hang comfortably empty by your sides, and take many other positions, according to the exercise.

Your eyes have only two positions: looking at the weight or looking straight ahead.

You look at the weight to see if you're holding it correctly. Concentrating on your grip helps you move confidently and smoothly through repetitions. With eyes connected to the weight you notice

Reverse grip

With eyes connected to the weight you notice
your own exertion.

your own exertion much better than if you are staring into space or glancing around at furniture that suddenly needs dusting and rearranging. Feeling your body working hard gives you an enhanced image of yourself, which leads to greater self-confidence in all daily tasks.

Looking straight ahead helps your balance while you exercise. And looking straight ahead into a mirror helps your ego! Your color is ruddy. Your complexion is improving. Your face has found new expressions to illustrate your powerful effort. You see your *form* for each exercise in the same way dancers see theirs when rehearsing in a mirror-lined room. You become more aware of your body's possibilities if you *watch* it progress through a program. You concentrate harder.

As a general rule, never look down at the floor while weight lifting. Looking down disrupts balance and rhythm.

Don't Waste Time Between Sets

When exercising with weights you are controlling two of the three factors that determine your strength: your emotional state and your training. (The third is heredity.) Willpower controls your emotions. You are using *willpower* to *train* every day. That willpower puts the weights through repetitions and gets you started once again after you rest between sets.

Willpower between sets is vital. Without it you lose concentration. You drop the barbell and pick up a spoon to stir a cake or feed the baby. You write letters mentally. You prowl from room to room, hunting for a moment's diversion. You read the newspaper and lose track of time. You rest longer each day.

Your resting period should be as short as possible—at most, one minute between sets. In this time you should not surrender to housework, entertainment, or excessive chatter with your partner. Instead, maintain a routine. Write down the number of repetitions done in each set. (Keep a notebook of your progress; include your body measurements and weight.) Breathe deeply and walk around the room so as not to cool off. Fight boredom by thinking about your goals, about your accomplishments so far, and about the exercise you will be starting next. Sixty seconds pass in no time.

Exercising offers no hiding place: you are either doing it or not. Your willpower must take you through the rests and back to the sets with no self-indulgent delays en route.

Warm Down Professionally

You put down the dumbbells after your final set of exercises. You put them away. Now what? A cold shower? A long nap? We advise a short warm-down comprised of the cross-crawl exercise (see illustration on p. 51) and a few stretching and bending exercises from Chapter 3. Another ideal warm-down is the rag doll: bend over from the waist and let your body hang as loose as possible. Shake your arms and hands. Let hands hang while you breathe completely out. Up and breathe in. Repeat several times.

If you have a spinal problem, these three warm-down "hangs" will traction the spine: hang from a chinning bar in your home gym or health club; hang upside down from the knees; hang in gravity boots. Hanging in gravity boots is the superior "hang" of the three. Although they look like horrific space gear, gravity boots provide the best means of stretching the body because you hang free in them, free and relaxed. You can't hang for long by your hands, knees, or feet because of the strain of gripping. Strain causes tension, the very opposite of a warm-down. Begin hanging in gravity boots for a minute or two at a time.

Stretching the spine is an excellent warm-down.

Hang in gravity boots from the chinning bar to warm down.

Gradually increase "hang-time" to five minutes.

Take a warm bath or shower to further relax your muscles.

Notice Your Side Benefits

While you are warming down, take time to notice any side benefits you may be receiving from exercising with weights. Those benefits listed below have been reported to us over the years by women following our programs. You might match your own self-discoveries with theirs.

1. Exercising with weights is a natural tranquilizer. Many women report their lives have become calmer since they began a Columbu program: they explain that they lose their tempers less frequently and are less often upset by home or office "catastrophes." They mention giving up their reliance on tranquilizing drugs after they have established a habit of weight training. They speak of a new feeling of well-being.
2. They also mention that they "sleep better": fall to sleep with ease and sleep soundly through the night.
3. Women who have always doubted their abilities as athletes say they now have a sport to be "good at." They mention their improved coordination, agility, and reflexes and their feelings of having achieved excellence in a field they had long given up on.
4. Many notice their "springier step," a new ease and grace in simply moving around the house and outdoors.
5. Their healthier hair, nourished by improved circulation, delights and surprises women in our programs.
6. Improved vision is reported by women who stay with weight ex-

ercising for six months or longer. Improved digestion is an almost immediate side benefit reported to us.
7. We are often told that a training session gives organization to an otherwise disorganized day, that the self-discipline of exercise carries over into other activities that might have been put off in the past because they were physically or mentally difficult. Women describe their confidence that derives from self-discipline.

Ignore Ridicule

Friends and relatives will begin to kid you even before you buy a set of weights. When you first mention your new exercise program you'll suddenly be "crazy." Everyone within hearing distance will make at least one disparaging comment. According to women who have sought our advice about training programs, kidding occasionally turns to ridicule when they bring weights home to establish a gym of their own. Now they are "masculine" and potentially "musclebound." Worse, they are "desperate."

We advise those who are unusually sensitive to such remarks to join a health club and work out in a group of supportive women. There is more than strength in numbers: there is peace of mind. We advise others to learn to live with ridicule. Withstanding it may be painful at first, but determination grows as weight lifting begins to work its magic. Progress obviously contradicts disapproval; ridiculers will want to "play" in your gym.

If you are convinced that weight training will help build you a stronger, sounder, healthier, more beautiful body, then continue with our programs no matter who says what. You will shortly prove with your own effort that muscles are neither "ugly" nor "foolish."

Training with weights is a natural tranquilizer.

6

Making Weight Training a Habit: Your Second Program

The joy of seeing and feeling your body advance to an intermediate program is a powerful reason to turn the pages of this chapter. With your educated imagination you sense the value of each exercise. You've done lifts like some of these already. You've taken some of these same positions. As you look at the photographs your body feels the moves. You're prepared for them. Your body is firmer; you see definition; you rarely notice stiffness in your joints or soreness in your muscles. You've improved your balance and agility. You're willing to take aim at further progress, which comes only from a more comprehensive program.

As with all the Columbu programs, our intermediate is based on these two important principles of conditioning and strengthening the body: (1) *specificity*—to improve a certain muscle, exercise *that* muscle; (2) *demand*—a substantial improvement comes about when the muscle is stressed beyond its normal limit. The fourteen exercises here work every muscle group in your body. As for stress, we have increased the amount of weight you will be lifting as well as the number of repetitions and sets to be

performed. At first you'll feel the demand. Later your body will adapt to our well-scheduled "doses" of stress.

We suggest again that you train at home. You need add only an adjustable incline bench to your equipment. If you decide to join a gym to train at the intermediate level, be sure to take along this program and follow it. Gym staffs often give helpful advice to beginners but work less effectively with advanced weight lifters, particularly women.

This program is designed for three times a week the first month (Monday, Wednesday, Friday or Tuesday, Thursday, Saturday). After the first month you can keep training on this same schedule or increase to four days a week (Monday, Tuesday, Thursday, Saturday). In six months advance to the power program if you wish to find your top strength.

Exercise 22: Bench Press

The bench press develops the pectoralis muscles. Most benches have stationary supports for weights (metal rods that are perpendicular to the bench, which are used to hold the weight when it is not being lifted), but such supports are not necessary.

Bench Press 22A

22B

Lie on the bench. Lift your barbell from the support or from the hands of a training partner, or hold it across your legs as you lie down. Bring barbell to chest area (22A), keeping the bar level across the chest, not the neck. Inhale as you lower the barbell or at the barbell's lowest point. Push up and exhale to completion phase (22B). Repeat.

Use 25 to 35 pounds for this exercise. Do 3 sets of 12 repetitions the first month. From then onward (up to six months) do 3 x 15. After six months, 4 x 15. Increase the barbell weight according to your own personal strength. To test for that, the barbell must *feel heavy* on your last repetitions. If it does not, add weight.

The pectoralis muscles support and lift the breasts. You will probably find the bench press to be one of your most satisfying exercises because of the warmth it brings to the entire torso.

Exercise 23: Incline Cross-Flys

Set the bench as shown in incline position. Using 10-pound dumbbells, start in position 23A. Elbows are bent. Inhale. Lift straight up (23B). Start crossing and exhale. Cross as in 23C, uncross, and come down at the same time to point 23A.

First month, do 2 x 15 with 10 pounds in each hand.
Second to sixth month, do 3 x 15 with more weight, as desired.
Incline cross-flys work the pectoralis muscles, triceps, and neck.

Incline Cross-Flys 23A

23B

23C

Exercise 24: One-Arm Row

The purpose of this exercise is to work the antagonist muscles to the chest muscles: the latissimus dorsi, trapezius, rhomboideus, levator scapulae, and all the minor muscles of the back. Your back gives strength to posture.

With one hand on the bench or on another support (to prevent spinal problems) and feet as shown in 24A, pull 10-pound weight to the height of 24B. Lower, pull. Breathe in as you pull up. Change hands and repeat the set of 15.

The first month, do 3 x 15.

Second month, 3 x 20 with a heavier dumbbell.
Third to sixth months, 4 x 20.

Exercise 25: Lateral Raises
(Same as Exercise 11)

Deltoids are the main muscles worked in this exercise. Lateral raises also stretch and tone neck muscles. Use a 10-pound dumbbell, one in each hand.

Do 2 x 15 the first month.
Do 3 x 15 the second.
After eight weeks, do 4 x 15 with more weight.

One-Arm Row 24A

24B

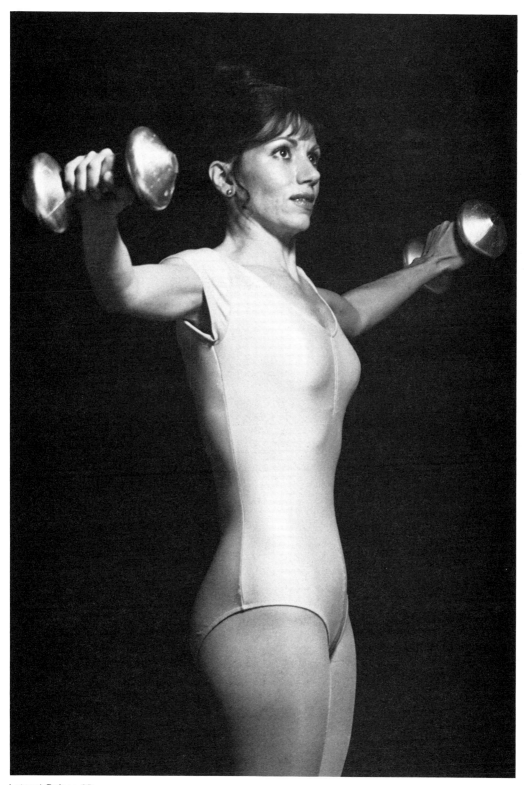

Lateral Raises 25

Front Raises 26A

Exercise 26: Front Raises

Again, deltoids are the prime movers. Your face muscles work during the many moments of effort in each repetition. This is Anita's favorite exercise for the upper arms.

With a 10-pound dumbbell in each hand, raise arms one at a time to the height shown. The complete range of motion is pictured in 26B.

Do 2 x 12 the first month.
Do 2 x 15 the second month.
After that add weight as desired and do 3 x 15.

Exercise 27: One-Arm Triceps Press
(Same as Exercise 12)

Strengthening the triceps helps you with many other exercises. For example, the triceps supports the elbow.

26B

Seated Dumbbell Curl 28A

First month, do 3 x 15 with a 10-pound dumbbell.

Second month, do 4 x 15.
After the second month, increase weight.

28B

Dumbbell Pull-Over 29A

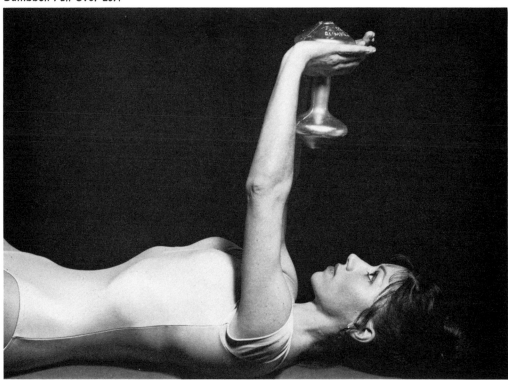

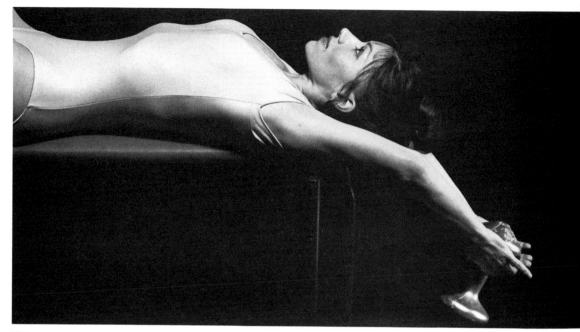

29B

Exercise 28: Seated Dumbbell Curl

Sit on a bench holding 10-pound dumbbells. Notice that the palms should be facing the body. Breathe in. As you lift the dumbbells, turn palms as shown in 28B. Exhale at top of lift. Curl to the height shown in 28B. Muscles worked in this exercise (biceps) are used in almost every physical act.

> First month, do 2 x 15 with 10-pound dumbbells.
> Second month, do 3 x 15.
> Stay with these numbers through the six-month program.

Exercise 29: Dumbbell Pull-Over

Dumbbell pull-overs stretch the rib cage and work the back, shoulders, and arms.

Lie on the bench, holding the dumbbell with straight arms. Lower dumbbell behind head as shown in 29B. As you lower you inhale; as you raise you exhale. You should lower as far as you can each repetition. Your range of motion will keep increasing over the months. When you stand up from this exercise you will notice immediately that you can stretch farther in all directions.

> First month, do 3 x 12 with a 15-pound dumbbell.
> Second month, do 3 x 15 with 20 pounds.
> After that, do 4 x 15 until the end of this program.

Barbell Squats 30A

Exercise 30: Barbell Squats

Thigh and calf muscles, gluteus medius, gluteus maximus, abdominals, and spinal muscles—the entire lower body —work during barbell squats.

Stand with your heels on blocks, barbell balanced as in 30A. Lower your body to position 30B. Raise. Lower. Continue. The squat feels more awkward

30B

than other exercises but after a few weeks your form improves and you will do squats with ease.

First month, 2 x 20 with 20–30 pounds.

Second month, do 3 x 20 with 30 pounds.

After that, increase the weight but not the repetitions.

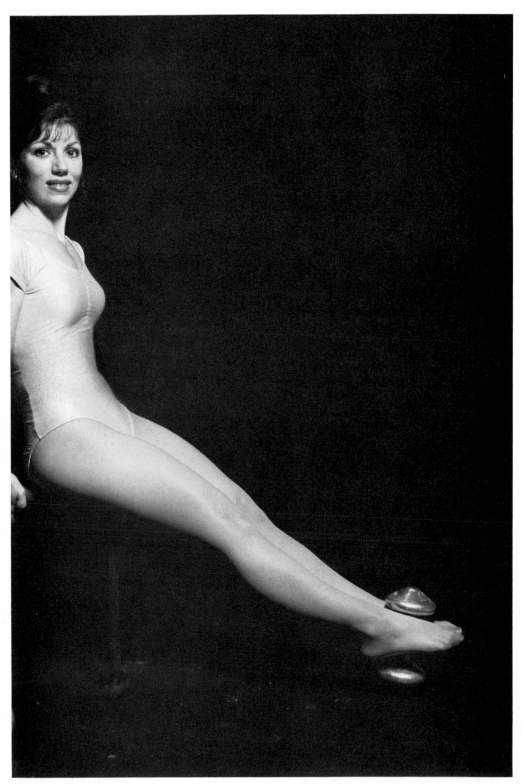

Leg Extensions 31

Exercise 31: Leg Extensions
(Same as Exercise 17)

This exercise strengthens quadriceps and abdominals. Also, as does almost any exercise for the legs, it will work your foot muscles.

First month do 2 x 20 with 20 pounds.
Second month, do 3 x 20 with 30 pounds.
Add weight after the eighth week and do 4 x 20. Increases in weight are usually made 10 pounds at a time.

Exercise 32: Leg Curl

Lie on your stomach on the bench. Hold onto the bench to stabilize your body. Lift dumbbell held between your feet to position 32B. This exercise stretches hamstring muscles, reduces fat in buttocks, and strengthens your lower back.

Do 2 x 15 the first month with 10 pounds.
Do 3 x 15 the second with 20 pounds.
Do 3 x 20 after that. Increase weights.

Leg Curl 32A

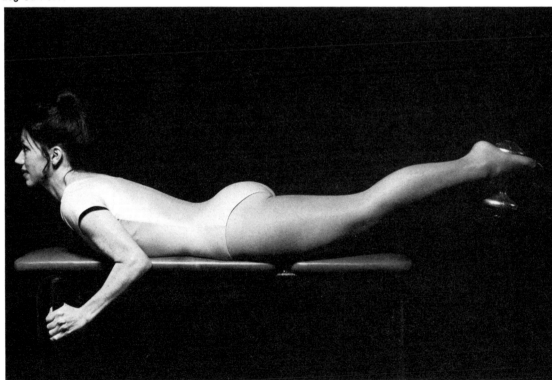

Exercise 33: Straight Leg Raises
(Same as Exercise 20)

These final three exercises are done without weights. Franco has discovered through years of training that working the abdominals with weights makes them bulge out of the stomach. Also, the waist thickens if worked with weights. By exercising without weights you'll keep those muscles shorter, higher, and tighter.

Follow the same instructions given in Exercise 20, only do more.
The first month, do 3 x 50 or 4 x 50.
Add as desired.

Exercise 34: Bent-Leg Sit-Ups
(Same as Exercise 19)

First month, 3 x 25.
Second month, 4 x 25.
Increase according to the progress you wish to make.

Exercise 35: Lying-Side Leg Raises
(Same as Exercise 6)

First month, do 4 x 50.
Second month, do 4 x 75.
Continue to add sets and repetitions if desired.

32B

As you add exercises and therefore time to your sessions you increase the problem of fitting your training into each day. Dramatic results have kept you going for some months, but as your improvement levels off you may feel less enthusiastic about expanding your program. In deciding whether to go on to the next chapter and add power to your already toned and strengthened body you might remember this forecast, based on our own experience as well as on research regarding power programs: progress seems to inch along after your various breakthroughs in the beginning and intermediate programs, but further breakthroughs will happen to place you on higher and higher performance levels of strength, endurance, and energy. Progress often comes in a rush after a long plateau. Also, with regard to muscles, there is no such thing as standing still. If you train you are progressing, however imperceptibly. If you stop training you slowly, slowly lose the muscle tone you've gained by hard work.

Straight Leg Raises 33

7

Strength: A Power Program for Women

Great feats of strength are common these days and have become an almost routine part of our spectator lives. Our entertainment is crowded with strongmen. They assemble on Saturday TV to bend iron bars with their bare hands and to carry refrigerators on their backs during foot races. The televised Olympics show us world-class weight lifters lifting 500 pounds with ease. Films about weight lifters and superstrong body builders attract increasingly large crowds. At your local health clubs there are bound to be a dozen heavy-lifters who could qualify for regional power-lifting meets. Many high school boys—and even junior high boys—are entering youth competitions at YMCAs and elsewhere. There they lift more pounds than did professional musclemen twenty-five years ago.

And women, too, are beginning to enter weight-lifting meets, to compete against men and other women. New research suggests that women have strength that is potentially as great, or greater than that of men, and more and more women are becoming interested in discovering just how much strength potential they have. We have all read about remarkable feats of strength performed by ordinary women in moments of great emotion. For instance, a 110-pound mother lifted a car off her child to save his life. An army nurse lifted an enormous bomb from a hospital garden to save her patients. Neither of these women was especially strong in the usual meaning of the word. In their normal state, a heavily loaded barbell would have stumped them. Without the emotional stress of impending death, their adrenal hormones would not have stimulated their metabolism to make possible greater and speedier liberation of energy.

Our purpose in this chapter is not to celebrate women's heroic strength in once-in-a-lifetime circumstances. Nor are we concerned with recruiting women for international power-lifting events. More and more women will certainly be competing in the future, as they will be in every sport that has previously been considered only for men. Our strength program (below) is not directed to these competitors. Rather, we are concerned with the women who followed our first program, improved through the intermediate program, and who now want to boost their power considerably: women who enjoy exercising with weights and wish to find their own peak performances.

Heroes are usually strong, but strength is not only for heroics. Strength is for every day. Strength is stamina is power is speed. If you begin thinking about the role of strength in your life you discover that almost every act can be made more simple by a superstrong body. You rise earlier, with energy left from the day before. Your legs swing out of bed, and as soon as your feet touch the floor you feel a flow of powerful motion. Leg strength will take you up and down stairs, up and down hills all day as if you were on level ground. Power in your back and forearms zips you through housework that you might have avoided in the past: a floor waxer becomes as light as a mop; storm windows and screens glide into place without help from a handyman; a refrigerator, a stove can be moved from a corner for cleaning underneath. Women who follow our strength program report that gardening rarely tires them, that they maneuver the lawnmower and other heavy equipment with no strain. At the office their strength is speed and stamina. Strong shoulders and forearms improve typing. Stamina allows you to go from meetings to business lunches and back to the office, with energy left when you get home at night. In jobs that were once held exclusively by men, women's muscles help them compete for entry and advancement. Firewomen, policewomen, army engineers, and dozens of other occupations are filled by those who pass strength tests.

Strength adds hours to your days. No matter what work you have done from 9:00 a.m. to 5:00 p.m. you are ready to change gears and play after eight hours. Your body stays loose enough for disco dancing or tennis. Your mind keeps alert to play bridge or to study for an exam. Strength is stamina, mental stamina as well as physical.

Not an hour goes by that the strong don't feel pleasure simply in living in their bodies. Strength feels good. It feels like a coiled spring that can contend with any circumstance. At the same time it makes the body feel as relaxed as if it were swinging in a hammock. That combination of power and poise can be noticed by tensing, then releasing any muscle group. Make a fist and flex your wrist. Muscles tighten in your arm. That small surge feels good. When you open your hand again, the tension release feels good, as well. Larger, stronger muscles feel better to tense and release, to stretch and relax, to move about solving physical problems. Knowing that you are unusually strong, remembering the power you have in reserve gives a steady feeling of confidence and pleasure through the day.

To progress in strength you must (1) add weight to your exercises; (2) increase the number of repetitions; (3) lessen the time you rest between sets. You must "overload" your muscles, forcing them to work harder. The exercises in this power program will not be instantly gratifying. Your body will immediately perceive the additional exertion. It will ask you to put the weights down, to rest, to take the exercises out of order, with the easier exercises first and the harder ones never. Your rebellious body will ask you to skip whole training sessions or to wait for a training partner you know will never arrive. Training partners will become harder to find as you lengthen and toughen your weight sessions. For this reason you may wish to join a health club, where partners are more readily available. Also, because you will be needing much heavier loads of weight, you will save the expense of improving your home gym by joining a club. You will add safety to your exercises by having spotters nearby to help you handle the weights in an emergency.

Local, national, and world-class power lifting lie beyond the exercises in this chapter. If you are on your way to those goals, the Columbu strength program is a reasonable way station. If you plan only to find and hold a high-powered strength performance, you can continue with only this program for years to come.

Here are three final tips for those in our strength program:

1. Never overtrain. Muscles become fatigued, which can result in a strain.
2. When tired, leave the gym. Most injuries occur on the final set.
3. Do not socialize while you are actually lifting heavy weights. Concentrate on the exercise to avoid injury.

(Do the following exercises three times per week: Monday, Wednesday, Friday or Tuesday, Thursday, Saturday.)

Exercise 36: Bench Press

The bench press is Franco's favorite. Along with the squat and the dead lift, it is one of the King Kongs of power training.

Bench press on the Universal machine, as shown here, or return to Exercise 22 and bench press with the barbell. The first two months, do 5 sets:

> 1 set of 12 repetitions with 20 pounds
> 1 set of 8 repetitions with 30 pounds
> 1 x 6 with 40 pounds
> 1 x 2 with 50 pounds
> 1 x 1 with the maximum you can lift

The second two months, increase to 6 sets:

> 1 set of 12 reps with 20 pounds to

Bench Press 36

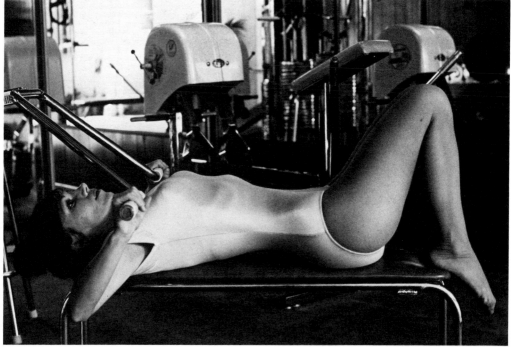

Incline Bench Press 37A

warm up
1 set of 6 reps with 40 pounds
1 x 4 with 50 pounds
1 x 1 with maximum you can lift
1 x 1 with maximum you can lift
1 x 1 with maximum you can lift

37B

Every second week test yourself for your maximum weight. Otherwise you will not know if you are getting stronger.

Exercise 37: Incline Bench Press

With your back supported by an incline bench, and holding the barbell as shown, lift barbell to position 37B. Breathe in as the weight is being lowered. Breathe out as you push up.

For the first two months, do 2 sets of 10 reps with what you can handle. (This means you should be able to finish the set but be almost completely worn out.) For the third set, add 10 pounds and do only 6 repetitions. For the fourth set, add another 10 pounds and do only 5 repetitions.

As time goes on, increase weights. Sets and repetitions stay the same.

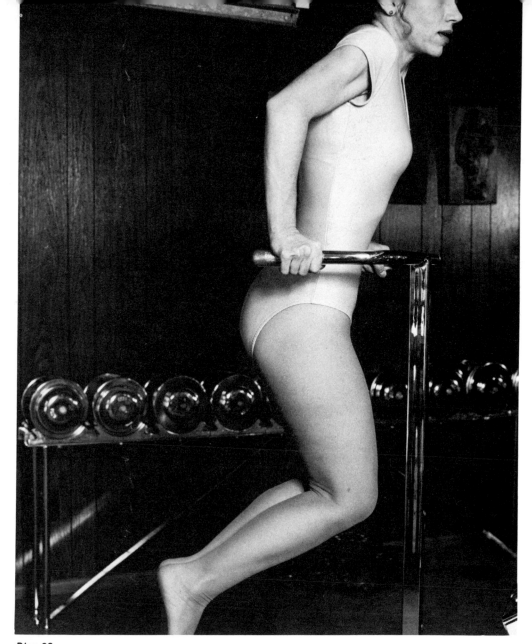

Dips 38

Exercise 38: Dips

For many women, dips seem one of the most difficult exercises. This is because women have *weak* triceps and pectorals *in proportion to their body weight*. Dips are easier for very slim women, for they simply have less weight to lift and lower.

Learning the form and a personal rhythm for dips makes them easier. Begin by lowering yourself just a little way,

about one-half the total range of motion. As your strength improves, do one-half the movement. As time goes by, the exercise becomes easier. Keep your head up and chest forward. For the first month, do 3 sets of 4 reps. After that, increase repetitions until you bring them up to 10. You will be working the lower pectoralis muscles, which lie directly under the breasts.

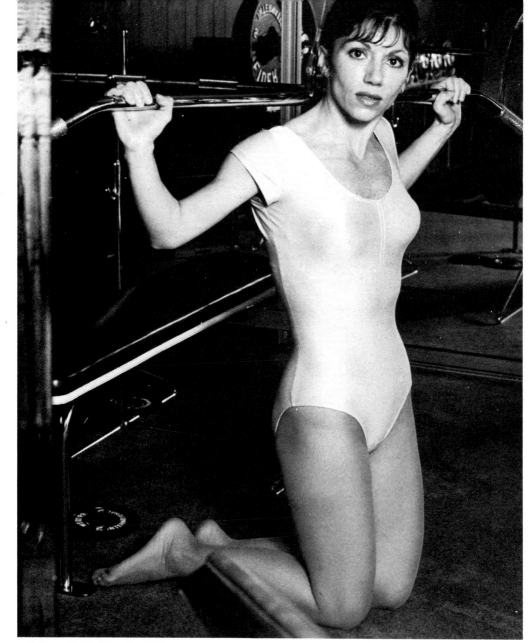

Pull-Down Behind the Neck 39

Exercise 39: Pull-Down Behind the Neck

The pull-down builds up all your major and minor back muscles, which in turn help the squat, the dead lift, and the bench press.

Kneeling on the floor, take the weight bar behind your neck as shown and pull it down as far as you can. Raise. (The bar raises itself on a pully when you release your downward pressure.) Pull down. Repeat. Exhale as you pull down.

Do 5 sets of 10 repetitions with the maximum weight you can pull down and still finish the set.

Front Pull-Down 40

Triceps Push-Down 41

Exercise 40: Front Pull-Down

The front pull-down exercises your back muscles from a different direction. Together with the behind-the-neck pull-down, it gives your back superpower and definition.

Kneeling on the floor, pull the weight bar from its top position to the upper chest, as shown in 40. Raise. Pull down. Do 5 sets of 10 repetitions at the maxi-mum weight you can handle for the 10 reps.

Exercise 41: Triceps Push-Down

Anita's picture is the starting position. Push the bar down until your arms are straight. Exhale as you push down for 5 sets of 10 repetitions at maximum weight. You are increasing your power for the bench press.

Exercise 42: Curl
(Same as Exercise 28)

To help you eke out an extra repetition or two, squeeze the dumbbells tight. Remember not to jerk the dumbbells. Move them smoothly for 2 sets of 10 repetitions with 15-pound dumbbells.

Exercise 43: Lateral Raises
(Same as Exercise 25)

Lateral raises will help you hold the squat bar better. Do 4 sets of 8 repetitions with 15- or 20-pound dumbbells. Add weight as desired.

Curl 42

Exercise 44: Barbell Squats
(Same as Exercise 30)

This is the most basic of all thigh exercises. The thighs, of course, are already your most powerful muscles, so we recommend squatting all the weight you can handle, as long as you increase properly. You can increase the weight for years.

Make certain your legs bend from the front, not with your knees going farther apart. To make sure of this, stand with your toes between 10 and 14 inches apart, but no more. Place the bar on your shoulders, not on your neck. If you hold the bar too high, you'll be placing too much weight on your spine. Use a wide grip, your hands close to the plates. And be sure to look straight ahead. This will keep you in better bal-

Barbell Squats 44A

44B

ance and your back straighter.
Your first two months, do 5 sets:

1 x 15 with 20 pounds
1 x 8 with 40 pounds
1 x 4 with 50 pounds
1 x 2 with 60 pounds
1 x 1 or 1 x 2 at maximum

If you are stronger than this, increase the weight accordingly. After eight weeks, bring the sets to 8. Increase the weight and do fewer repetitions.

Exercise 45: Leg Press
Sit and press the pedals of the leg press. Use your whole foot or only your toes, whichever feels comfortable. Breathe out as you push. Do 3 sets of 8 reps with *heavy weight* (about 85 percent of your maximum).

Leg Press 45

Leg Extension 46

Exercise 46: Leg Extension

Sit on the leg-extension machine. Holding onto the bench firmly, lift the weight bar to maximum extension. Use medium speed. Flex your thighs at the same time you do this exercise. When the bar is all the way up, keep thighs flexed for 2 seconds, then go all the way down.

Start with 5 sets of 15 reps at a weight that makes your legs burn on the final 3 repetitions. Build up the weight every month.

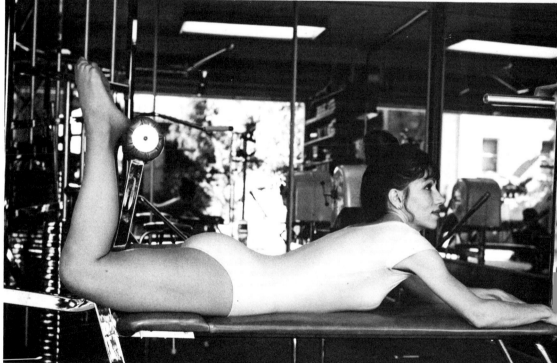

Leg Curl 47A 47B

Exercise 47: Leg Curl

Start as shown in 47A. Hold the bench firmly, curl to position 47B. The first two months, do 2 x 15. After that, do 3 x 15. Use 10 pounds at first and build up.

Legs curls are the best thigh biceps exercise. Straighten your legs completely on the way down; try to touch your thighs on the way up. Your action must be fluid, without jerking, in order to affect the thigh biceps.

Dead Lift 49A

49B

Exercise 48: Calf Raises
(Same as Exercise 18)

If your gym has a calf-raise machine, use that. Wearing shoes, stand very straight on the machine. Go all the way up and all the way down.

Or do calf raises as described in Exercise 18. Do 5 x 15 with heavy weights. You'll never get powerful calves with light weights.

Exercise 49: Dead Lift

With knees bent, grip the barbell with one hand overgrip, one hand undergrip. Look straight ahead. Lift barbell from the floor to position 49B. Exhale as you lift. You are strengthening your back, legs, and your grip.

For the first two months, do up to 5 sets, starting with 40–50 pounds. Increase 10 pounds every set as you reduce repetitions: first set, 6 reps; second, 4 reps; third, 2 reps; fourth set, 1 rep; fifth set, 1 rep.

Incline Sit-Ups 50

Exercise 50: Incline Sit-Ups

Set the board at a 25-degree angle. With knees bent, sit up from the lying-down position. The abdominals are worked only to sit-up point, as shown in picture, so sitting up higher is wasteful of energy and sometimes causes lower-back problems.

For the first two months, do 3 x 10. After that, do 4 x 25 or 4 x 30.

Exercise 51: Straight Leg Raises
(Same as Exercises 20 and 33)

Do the same number as in Exercise 33 unless your abdominals have been slow to make progress. In that event, do more sets and reps.

Lock your knees, point your toes, raise and lower your legs without moving your hips.

Exercise 52: Lying-Side Leg Raises
(Same as Exercises 6 and 35)

Do the same number as in Exercise 35.

8

Specialization: Weight Exercises for Specific Problems

Women often ask our help about special problem parts of their bodies, parts that are slower than other muscle groups in responding to a beginning weight program (Chapter 4). They tell us that they do their exercises precisely as we describe them but that "nothing works" on their thighs, buttocks, or breasts, or on their lower back, which continues to ache.

Suppose you have such a problem part. Suppose further that your slow-to-respond part is one you are eager to exercise into premier condition—for proportionate development and for better health. You have *always* wanted firmer thighs. You're tired of slumpy buttocks. You're sick of back pains. What to try next?

We suggest that you continue with our beginning program until you have completed it (according to our instructions on pages 27–46). Start the next day on our intermediate program (Chapter 6) and follow it for a week, until you have settled into the pattern and rhythm of exercises and find each session that the new muscles you are working feel less sore than the day before. At this point, look carefully at your thighs (or but-

tocks, etc.). Measure them with a tape measure. Flex and feel for muscle tone. You may notice a satisfying firmness, which will forecast even greater improvement during the intermediate program. But again, you may not be pleased with your progress. Your thighs may not have come near the standard you set for them when you bought weights. What to try now?

An immediate breakthrough level of tone, size, and therefore proportion is sure to result from specialization. You must lengthen your training sessions and add extra exercises for thighs (or buttocks, etc.). Numerous sets of high repetitions with medium weights would correct certain problems in short order, but we do not recommend this approach. Your specialization should be kept within bounds of your overall progress: highly developed thighs would seem out of place atop spindly calves. For such total-body development along with specialization we suggest this program:

1. From the exercises below, select two or three that influence your problem area.

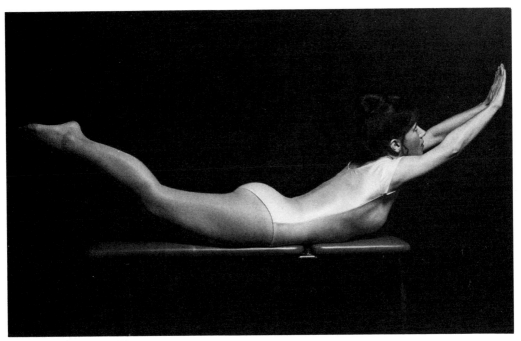

Super-hyperextension 53

2. Begin each daily workout with these. That way your energy is highest for your priority exercises. Also, you have more oxygen in your bloodstream, which causes the muscles to grow more. If you add specialization exercises to the end of your intermediate program you may well be too tired to do them with vigor.

3. After two weeks, return to your regular all-around schedule for a breather. Assess your progress and repeat your specialization exercises every two weeks for two weeks.

In Chapter 1 we mentioned spinal problems that trouble a large number of Americans. Unless you have suffered a traumatic injury (a strain or sprain, for example), spinal problems usually begin as stiffness and muscle soreness in the low back or neck. As time passes, pain gradually increases. Muscles become tighter and weaker; eventually they begin pulling the vertebrae out of alignment. When this happens there is pressure on spinal nerves. Pain becomes more intense, although for a while it comes and goes. Later, pain becomes chronic and is often accompanied by other symptoms: numbness, tingling, burning skin, for example.

Many spinal problems can be prevented, particularly those that occur because of weak muscles. Proper exercise strengthens back muscles, which then keep the body in alignment. Our exercise programs are meant to strengthen *all* of your body's muscles. If your spinal problems are minor they will probably disappear after several months' training. To insure extra strength in your back muscles or to combat early warnings of possibly chronic problems, we suggest that you choose several special back exercises (below) to add to your intermediate program.

Rocking Back 54

Knee to Chest 55

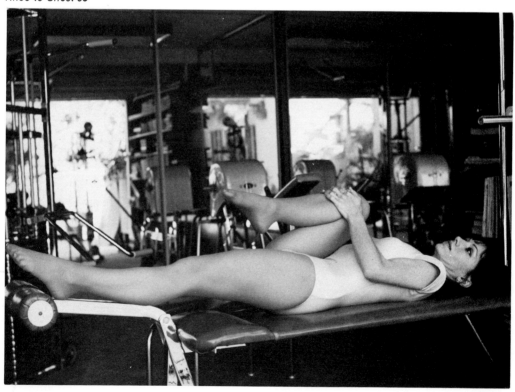

Exercise 53: Super-Hyperextension

Lie face down on a bench or on the floor. Lift feet and arms to Anita's position in 53. Get a maximum stretch, relax down, come back up. Super-hyperextension reduces spinal tension and strengthens lower spinal muscles. Add 2 sets of 10 repetitions to your program.

Exercise 54: Rocking Back

Start on the floor or on a bench. Take hold of your legs with your hands (as in photo). While you are holding them, try to rock back and forth. Over several weeks, this exercise becomes easier. You'll start with a tight, short rock but soon achieve complete range of motion. Do 2 sets of 10 repetitions.

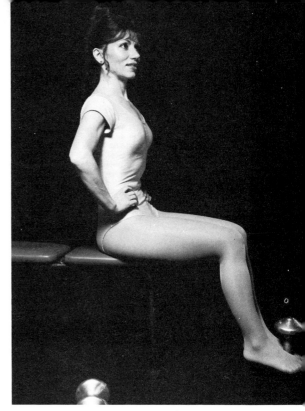

Leg Extensions 56A

56B

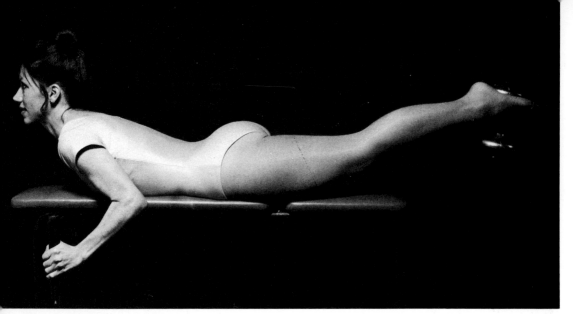

Leg Curl 57A

Exercise 55: Knee to Chest

Lying on a bench or on the floor, take hold of your knee as shown. Pull your knee to the chest and hold it 10 seconds. Release, repeat with the opposite leg. Do at least 10 of these.

The next three exercises are for problem thighs. These will tighten without adding bulk.

Exercise 56: Leg Extensions
(Same as Exercise 17)

Using no more than 10 pounds of weight, do 3 x 30.

Exercise 57: Leg Curl
(Same as Exercise 32)

Do 2 x 30 with 10 pounds.

Exercise 58: Lying-Side Leg Raises
(Same as Exercise 6)

Do 3 x 100 on each side.

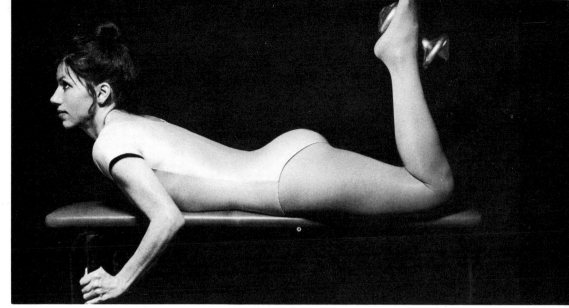

57B

These next two exercises will trim and firm buttocks. They should bring results within a few weeks.

Exercise 59: Barbell Squats
(Same as Exercises 30 and 44)
Using 20–30 pounds on the barbell, do 3 sets of 25 repetitions.

Exercise 60: Back Leg Stretch
(Same as Exercise 8)
Do 3 x 20 with each leg.

Back Leg Stretch 60A
60B

If you believe that your breasts are too small, do the following:

Exercise 61: Bench Press
(Same as Exercises 22 and 36)
   Do 4 x 12 at 20–30 pounds.

If you believe your breasts need firming and raising, do the following:

Exercise 62: Cross-Flys
(Same as Exercise 9)
   Do 3 x 30 with 5-pound dumbbells.

Bench Press 61A

61B

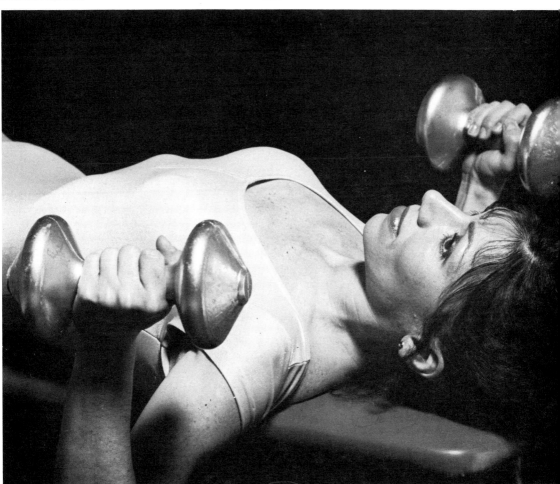

Cross-Flys 62A

62B

9

Weight Training for Improvement in Sports

If you have always played a sport but never trained with weights, be prepared for a pleasant shock: you will make sudden, dramatic progress in your sport shortly after beginning the first Columbu program.

Muscle strength gives you an advantage in sports because it's an important basis for endurance and power (strength plus speed). As you increase your strength you also improve your balance, agility (the ability to change directions rapidly while moving fast), coordination, quickness (reaction time), and speed. Of course each of the Columbu programs, even Chapter 3, will make you stronger as well as help to trim your excess fat: stored fat limits an athlete's performance.

In order to use weight training to help you as an athlete pinpoint a skill used in your sport that you want to improve. Your swimming backstroke, for example, or your tennis backhand. Then, using knowledge gained so far in our exercise programs, decide which of your muscle groups specifically need to be strengthened to help each skill. Let's take these two examples that may start you thinking about your own sport. The back-stroke in swimming is beautiful but difficult because the body must keep high in the water. Your backstroke form and speed will depend in part on strong lower-back muscles. You have already been introduced to hyperextensions (Exercise 7) for the lower back, and this exercise will help to strengthen those important muscles. As for your tennis backhand, an increase in forearm strength will improve racket-preparation efficiency and racquet control both on impact and during the follow-through. The forearm flexors can be strengthened by doing wrist curls (Exercise 13), so add extra wrist curls to your beginning or intermediate weight program.

For this chapter we have selected fourteen sports popular with women today. For each sport we have matched a basic skill or skills with the specific muscle or muscle groups needed to be strengthened for improvement in the skill. Further, we have suggested a weight exercise that works directly on the muscle identified. Our chapter is nothing like a complete catalogue of sports exercises. We offer the following merely to prompt your own thinking and further reading about your own sports and muscles. After you reach decisions, add those weight exercises to your beginning or intermediate programs.

Exercise 63: Jumping Rope for Bicycling
Bicycling calls, of course, for strong legs. We suggest jumping rope, which works on every leg muscle. For two months, do 3 sets of 2 minutes each. Rest no more than one minute between sets. After two months, increase to 3 sets of 3 minutes each and increase your jumping speed. Do this four times a week.

Exercise 64: Reverse Barbell Curls for Bowling
Reverse curls quickly build the forearm so a smooth pendulum motion of the ball can be made for increased accuracy.
Begin with arms and barbell straight down in front of you. Raise them *through* the position shown until arms are in front of your neck, barbell shoulder high. Lower. Raise.

Do 3 x 10, three times a week.
Use 25 to 30 pounds.

Exercise 65: Squats for Cross-Country Skiing
The muscles most important to cross-country skiing are the leg muscles. With these you maintain balance, maintain weight over the skis, stabilize legs and knee joints, etc.
Holding barbell as shown, squat to position 65B, up, squat again. Look straight ahead.

Do 4 x 12, two to' three times each week.
Use 30 to 50 pounds.

Jumping Rope for Bicycling 63

Reverse Barbell Curl for Bowling 64

Squats for Cross-Country Skiing 65A

Exercise 66: Dumbbell Swing for Golf

Swings are wonderful for elbows, which help maintain club control and give power on impact with the ball. Swings also loosen back muscles.

Starting in position 66A, swing dumbbell in position 66B. Swing back, swing forward, as shown.

Do 2 x 12, three times a week.
Use 20 pounds at first and increase over several months.

Exercise 67: Clean and Press for Hiking, Climbing, and Backpacking

Legs, arms, shoulders, back—everything needs strengthening for hiking endurance, especially if you will be carrying a heavy backpack over long distances. The clean and press is a blockbuster exercise that is perfectly possible for women to do. It conditions the entire body.

Using an overhand grip, lift the barbell from position 67A through 67C.

Do 3 x 12, twice a week.
Use 20 to 40 pounds.

65B

Dumbbell Swing for Golf 66A

66B

Clean and Press for Hiking, Climbing, and Back-packing 67A

67B

67C

Triceps Extension for Racquet Games 69

Exercise 68: Leg Press for Ice Skating and Roller Skating
(Same as Exercise 45)
Strong buttocks and quadriceps are developed by the leg press.

Do 3 x 15, twice a week.
Use heavy weight because your legs are already strong: 40 to 60 pounds.

Exercise 69: Triceps Extension for Racquet Games
Strong triceps allow you to hit the ball hard, especially when serving. They improve your follow-through and help prevent elbow injury.
From the position shown, extend the arms until straight. Return them to position 69.

Do 3 x 12, three times each week.
Use 10 to 15 pounds.

Exercise 70: Running for Racquet Games
A daily conditioning program of running several miles will increase your aerobic power and hence your stamina during racquet games.

Exercise 71: Calf Raises for Running
(Same as Exercise 18)

Do 4 x 15, three times a week.
Use slightly heavier weight than for Exercise 18.

Running for Racquet Games 70

Exercise 72: Leg Extensions for Skiing and Water Skiing
(Same as Exercise 46)

Leg extensions work the quadriceps, which absorb shock on landing on skis.
Do 4 x 15, three times a week.
Use same weight as recommended in Exercise 46.

Exercise 73: Upright Rowing for Swimming

With hands spaced 6 inches apart, use overhand grip to pick up the barbell. Pull the bar up to your chin and lower it to thigh level again. Pull up, lower. Anita's photograph shows her at almost the top position.

Muscular endurance will be developed through hours of water work and by weight training for arm pull and leg action. With upright rowing you strengthen your shoulders for all swimming strokes.

Do 3 x 10, twice a week.
Use 20 to 30 pounds.

Exercise 74: Seated Press Behind the Neck for Basketball

This exercise works the upper back, deltoids, and triceps, which in turn increase the distance you will be able to throw, pass, and shoot the basketball. If your arms and shoulders are strong, your shooting capability will not be affected by muscle fatigue in the game's second half.

Press the barbell from the position shown until the arms are completely straight. Barbell will be above *and* behind the neck.

Do 3 x 10, twice a week.
Use 20 to 30 pounds.

Leg Extensions for Skiing and Water Skiing 72

Seated Press Behind the Neck for Basketball 74

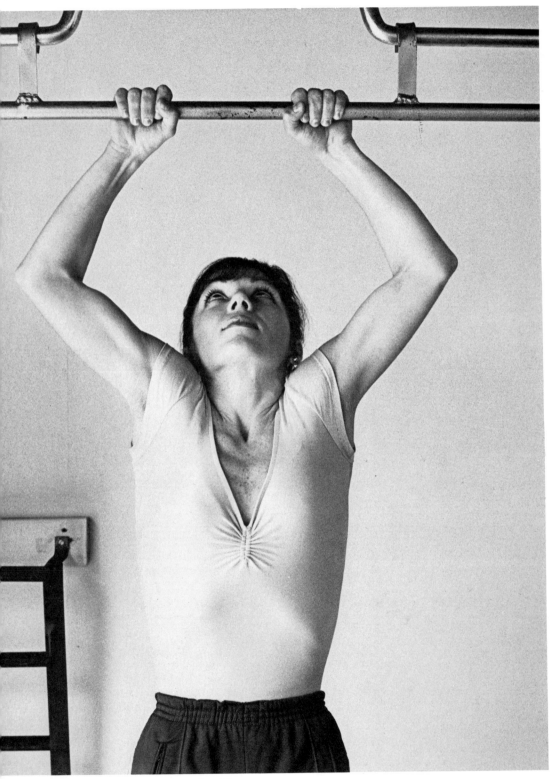

Narrow-Grip Chins for Field Hockey 75

Exercise 75: Narrow-Grip Chins for Field Hockey

Stickwork can be improved by strengthening the biceps and the latissimus dorsi muscles. Narrow-grip chins work these muscles strenuously. If your gym doesn't have the apparatus you see in the photograph, perform chins with your hands about 6 inches apart, or even overlapping, on a regular chinning bar. Pull up all the way, till the hands touch the chest if you can. Let down until your arms are fully extended. This is hard but possible.

Do 4 x 8, twice a week.

Exercise 76: Close-Grip Bench Press for Softball

Your grip should be no wider than 6 inches. In this style you work the triceps more than the pectoralis muscles. Triceps give explosive power to both throwing and hitting.

From the starting position shown, raise the barbell straight up to arms' length. Return it to chest and push up again. Don't arch your back.

Do 4 x 10, twice a week.
Use 15 to 25 pounds.

Close-Grip Bench Press for Softball 76

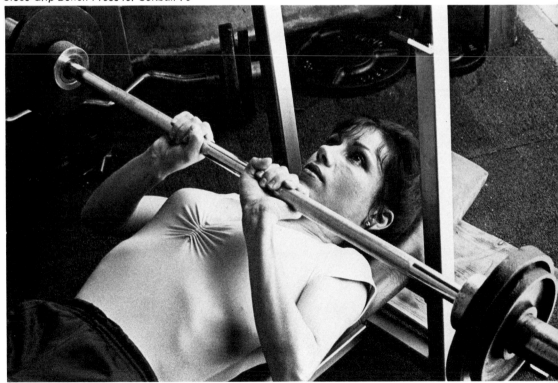

Bent-Over Barbell Rowing for Volleyball 77

Exercise 77: Bent-Over Barbell Rowing for Volleyball

Volleyball demands a high level of back strength used in spiking and blocking the ball. Bent-over rowing improves these defensive abilities.

Using a medium-width grip, palms down, lean over and let the bar hang, then bring it up to your chest. Lower. Repeat.

Do 3 x 10, twice a week.
Use 20 to 30 pounds.

10

Eating and Exercise

"How do you stay so slim?"

This is the question most frequently asked me by my women patients. I am always amused because for many years I was overweight and flabby and I still have twinges of a "fat complex."

I went through the usual fad diets and even tried health and beauty spas. After each attempt I eventually regained the weight I had lost, and even when I kept weight off for months at a time I still "looked fat" because of all the flab on my thighs and hips. When Franco and I met he tried to interest me in weight training, but I kept finding excuses for not following his programs on a regular basis. I tried exercising sporadically, but never saw any visible results. I worked hard adjusting patients in my chiropractic office and that seemed enough exercise. Besides, I felt tired from ten hours at the office. I hadn't enough energy to commute to a gym.

Franco didn't give up on weight lifting to solve my weight problem. Each time I complained about flab he suggested training. He gave me several health club memberships, but I stayed too busy to go regularly. Finally Franco constructed a gym at home, and all my excuses deteriorated. I began training and saw re-

sults in the mirror and on the scales almost immediately. Soon assured that weights worked, I arranged my schedule to include training at least four days a week. Positive changes in my body followed: my energy and stamina improved drastically; I became happier because I looked and felt so much better; I no longer resented Franco's long hours of training, for now I had a better understanding of his programs and goals; I lost weight and flab *for good.*

Combined with proper eating habits, weights work for good. When I was fat and trying all types of crash diets I also started researching my own diet problem. I wanted to find out why I was a slow, spasmodic loser, as were (and are) many of my patients. The main points I discovered are the following: women's hormonal balance changes each month, and as our bodies go through cycles, they must be continually supplied with optimum nutrients. Many women are constantly going on and off currently popular diets. This sort of dieting robs the body of vital nutrients, and over a period of weeks, months, and years can create a metabolic dysfunction. When the metabolism no longer functions normally (becomes hypometabolic), most

By combining proper nutritional habits with weight training you can be thin for life.

women still continue to go on and off diets. Some women also take reducing medication that complicates their problems even more. Often such dieting is not accompanied by exercise because women are fatigued, nervous, and without willpower to participate in sports and games. When dieting becomes unbearable they quit and gorge themselves, starting the cycle again. Hormonal changes combined with metabolic alterations caused by errors in diet can also cause frequent drastic mood changes.

Franco and I discourage our patients from dieting. Instead we urge them to learn to select foods which will supply all the nutrients necessary for good health and to eat these foods in moderation. Learning to eat properly and *not to overeat* can solve almost anyone's weight problem for a lifetime. (By "weight problem" we are also referring to those who are underweight.) Frequently, underweight women overload their systems with unhealthy amounts of sugar and other rich foods. We teach our patients the difference between artificial and natural foods. Many of them prefer to eat foods that come in a box, jar, or can because they lack time to shop for and prepare food from scratch. We stress that the extra time spent is time creating a starbody.

For weight loss and weight maintenance, breakfast is the most important meal. Don't skip breakfast. It should be a low-fat, moderate-protein, and natural-carbohydrate meal. Recent research has shown that upon eating the "average American breakfast," which is a high-sugar, highly refined carbohydrate breakfast (orange juice, coffee, donuts or sweet rolls), the blood sugar rises within fifteen minutes from a low-fasting blood sugar of 70 or 80 milligrams percent to around 130 to 140. (Normal is between 80 and 120.) Then, rather

quickly, the blood sugar plummets. It is your normal blood sugar that helps take away your sense of hunger, irritability, and fatigue. If you eat very lean protein and whole natural carbohydrates for breakfast, as well as for other meals, insulin is required to be secreted gradually and in a sense trickles into the bloodstream. It properly utilizes the blood sugar so that a blood-sugar level close to normal is maintained for hours. The research mentioned showed that we should eat about 35 grams of high-quality lean protein for breakfast, along with unprocessed carbohydrates in order to maintain a sufficiently high *prolonged blood sugar,* thus preventing fatigue and promoting efficiency during the day.

We do not advise the use of protein powder, protein tablets, or liquid protein. Our best advice is to keep your diet as natural and as simple as possible. Below are our specific recommendations for what should be included in your nutritional program.

Bread: We use pita bread or seven-grain, stoneground bread. Read labels and select a bread that contains no sugar or additives.

Grains: We eat raw bran flakes daily and always try to use natural whole grains that are not processed or refined. Natural brown rice is an excellent food.

Cereals: We have found seven-grain granola cereals to be the most nutritious. They are an excellent source of minerals and B-complex vitamins. Those overweight should eat cereal only one time per day.

Raw Seeds and Nuts: These supply essential fatty acids and are high in trace minerals and the B-complex vitamins. The underweight may nibble freely on all types of raw nuts. Nuts are high in calories and should not be eaten in excess if you are overweight.

Milk: We use low-fat milk for making

the yogurt that we eat daily. We prefer eating yogurt to drinking milk because the microorganisms that ferment milk into yogurt continue their activity in the intestinal tract and contribute to the body's manufacture of essential vitamins. Yogurt is also easier for some people to digest and assimilate.

Eggs: We use fertile eggs, but not more than one per day. Eggs are among the most nutritious foods on earth but are relatively high in fats.

Cheese: Cheese is an excellent source of protein but contains much fat. If you are overweight, use skim-milk cheese or low-fat cheese. Always eat whole, unprocessed cheese in preference to the types you can buy in tubes, cans, or jars. Cheese mixtures are chemically contaminated, so learn to read labels.

Poultry: Try to get poultry that is grown without any hormones or other injections. Health food stores often have it. Remove the skin before cooking, because the skin is high in fats. The most nutritious way to prepare poultry is to bake or broil it with vegetable seasonings.

Meat: Again, try to buy meat that is grown without any added hormones. Be sure to trim all visible fat before cooking. Eliminate fatty meats and eat only lean cuts of beef, lamb, and veal.

Soups: After cooking soup, cool and place it in the refrigerator. When the soup is cold, skim off the fat. Then reheat and you have a low-fat soup. Creamed soups (soups in which white flour and other refined carbohydrates have ben used) should be eliminated from your diet.

Seafood: Seafoods in general are low in fats, high in protein and in essential amino acids. They are especially high in trace minerals. We eat fresh fish several times each week. If you eat canned fish, it should be water-packed.

Oils and Fats: We try to eliminate all fried foods, all mayonnaise, all margarine, and almost all oils and oil dressings. The exception is that we do use small amounts of pure olive oil as salad dressing. When eating in restaurants we do not use any type of salad dressing because they are high in calories.

Fruits and Fruit Juices: Eat fresh fruit two or three times daily, as a snack or with meals. When possible, choose one *citrus* daily and choose *raw fruit*. Those overweight should avoid dried fruit because of the high sugar and calorie content. We believe that it is better to eat the whole fruit rather than drinking fruit juice because whole fruit adds bulk to the diet. However, fruit juice may replace one serving of fresh fruit daily. Fruit juice should always be made fresh.

Vegetables: You should eat three or more servings of fresh vegetables each day. We eat a large raw vegetable salad twice a day and lightly steamed vegetables twice a day, with an occasional baked potato. Do not overcook vegetables because they lose their nutritional value. Vegetables and fruits are rich in vitamins and minerals and are an excellent source of bulk when eaten raw. We must have bulk in our diet for proper intestinal function. The seven-grain cereals are also good forms of bulk.

Beverages: Use water, mineral water, herbal teas, milk, white wine (small amount), coffee substitutes (from health food stores) rather than decaffinated or instant coffee. Coffee and tea should be eliminated. We buy mineral water by the case and use it abundantly.

Foods to Avoid: Food preservatives such as nitrates and nitrites; sugar, white flour, hydrogenated fat; artificial coloring and flavoring. Although you may not be able to eliminate totally these "foods," it is possible to cut their use in your diet by taking the time to read labels and preparing your own fresh food. Sugar is perhaps the most potentially damaging item on this list. Recent research is beginning to link high sugar intake with muscular weakness, diabetes, hypoglycemia, dental cavities, kidney stones, urinary infections, cardiovascular disease, intestinal cancer, diverticulosis, indigestion, and hormone disorders, and of course it does nothing for those who are overweight.

Be aware of what you are eating daily. Before putting anything into your mouth, ask yourself what that food will do for your body. Try to schedule your meals at the same time each day, and weigh yourself at the same time on the same scale each day. Then try to take the extra weight off *that day,* which will help you to avoid accumulating extra pounds. Eat sitting down at the table, never standing in front of the sink, stove, or refrigerator.

Following these nutritional tips will start you on a lifetime pattern of eating for health.

11

The Shortest Program Ever Written

Almost everyone who has ever started a self-improvement program has at some point taken a short layoff or a long vacation from their regimen. Or quit altogether. Crash diets are perhaps the most quickly strayed from, but any sort of diet is usually dropped in favor of a few days' gorging. Exercise programs have their dropouts by the millions. Starting and stopping and restarting and quitting happens to those with the best intentions, the most compelling goals, and the most bothersome body conditions to correct. And of course few dropouts are more guilt-ridden than those from weight exercising. They regret their health club payments. The investment in a home set of weights is especially haunting. If only they'd dropped out of running: they could still wear their new striped shoes for a Saturday sport. But those dumbbells and barbells serve only one purpose. Plus they are huge and heavy—hard to bury and forget in a closet. Sure, dumbbells may have cost less than running shoes, but what good are they now?

They are still as good as the day they were brought home in eager expectation of the superb body they would help to form. They provide the fastest, surest way of slimming, toning, and strengthening *any* body. If brought out of the closet once again, even after a month or more gathering dust, they can be pressed into service *without starting all over again at the absolute bottom level of free exercising.*

The program in this chapter is a shortcut back to the beginning and intermediate levels in earlier chapters. Suppose you have been faithfully following the weight exercises in Chapter 4 or in Chapter 6. Then, for one reason or another, you stopped. You caught a bad cold; or you went away on vacation; or you unexpectedly missed a workout. Then another. You thought another day wouldn't make a difference until a week passed—and a week seemed a big difference. Now you're too discouraged to continue. Two weeks have passed.

Instead of burying your weights, return to Chapter 4 or to Chapter 6 (wherever you quit) by the shortcut below. By shortcut we mean that the quickie program is comprised of only a few exercises but that each exercise is demanding, designed to get your muscles up to par in the shortest amount of time. Do

Best of all, lifting feels good.

the first four exercises in the order presented. Do them swiftly and get them over with. After three days of the shortcut, return to your beginning weight program. Follow that program for a week, doing all of the exercises for seven days in a row, then return to the intermediate program. The second set of exercises given below is designed for women who are working to reduce their body weight. Do them in addition to the first four. In a pinch for time you can move rapidly through this routine each night just before going to bed.

Our shortcut can be substituted for your regular workout on days when you feel unusually rushed for time. But save these exercises for such emergencies. If you form a shortcut habit you have no further line of retreat when for some reason you quit training altogether for several weeks.

Columbu Shortcut

Exercise 1: Bench Press (Exercise 36)
Do 2 sets of 15 repetitions with 20 pounds.
Exercise 2: One-Arm Row (Exercise 24)
Do 2 sets of 15 repetitions with 10 pounds.
Exercise 3: Barbell Squats (Exercise 44)
Do 2 sets of 15 repetitions with 20 pounds.
Exercise 4: Lying-Side Leg Raises (Exercise 6)
Do 2 sets of 50 repetitions.

Add these if you are working to control or reduce your body weight.

Exercise 5: Bent-Leg Raises (Exercise 4)
Do 2 sets of 20 repetitions.
Exercise 6: Back Leg Stretch (Exercise 8)
Do 2 sets of 15 repetitions.

20 Week Progress Chart

	Start	1st week	3rd week	5th week	7th week	9th week	11th week	13th week	15th week	17th week	19th week	Goal
Upper arms												
Forearms												
Bust												
Waist												
Abdomen												
Hips												
Thighs												
Calves												
Weight												

Index

Note: Page numbers in **boldface** indicate illustrations